P9-CQC-680

Pattern-Oriented
Memory Forensics

Dmitry Vostokov
Software Diagnostics Institute

Published by OpenTask, Republic of Ireland

Copyright © 2014 by OpenTask

Copyright © 2014 by Software Diagnostics Institute

Copyright © 2014 by Software Diagnostics Services

Copyright © 2014 by Dmitry Vostokov

All rights reserved. No part of this book may be reproduced, stored in a retrieval system, or transmitted, in any form or by any means, without the prior written permission of the publisher.

You must not circulate this book in any other binding or cover and you must impose the same condition on any acquirer.

Product and company names mentioned in this book may be trademarks of their owners.

OpenTask books and magazines are available through booksellers and distributors worldwide. For further information or comments send requests to press@opentask.com.

A CIP catalogue record for this book is available from the British Library.

ISBN-l3: 978-1-908043-76-4 (Paperback)

First printing, 2014

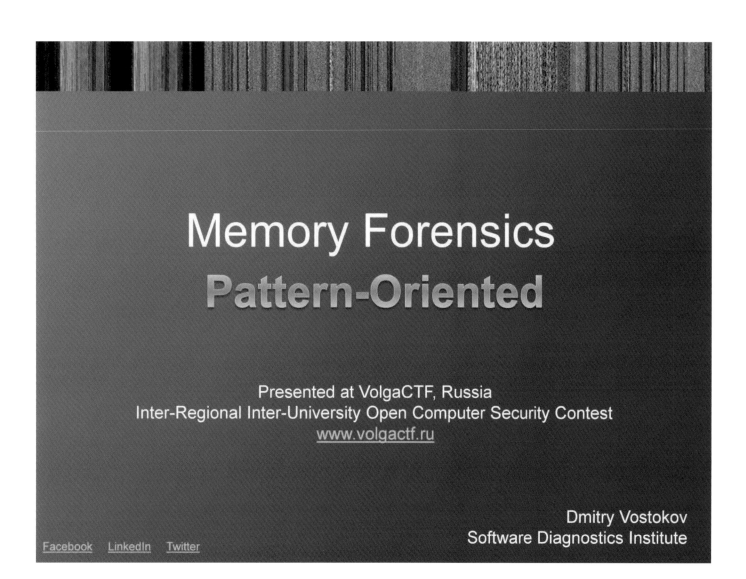

Hello Everyone, my name is Dmitry Vostokov and I introduce today a pattern language for memory forensics. First we start with a short theoretical part, provide a few definitions, and then we illustrate the pattern-oriented approach with a few crash dump analysis examples by using WinDbg debugger from Microsoft Debugging Tools for Windows.

Facebook:
http://www.facebook.com/DumpAnalysis

LinkedIn:
http://www.linkedin.com/in/vostokov

Twitter:
http://twitter.com/DumpAnalysis

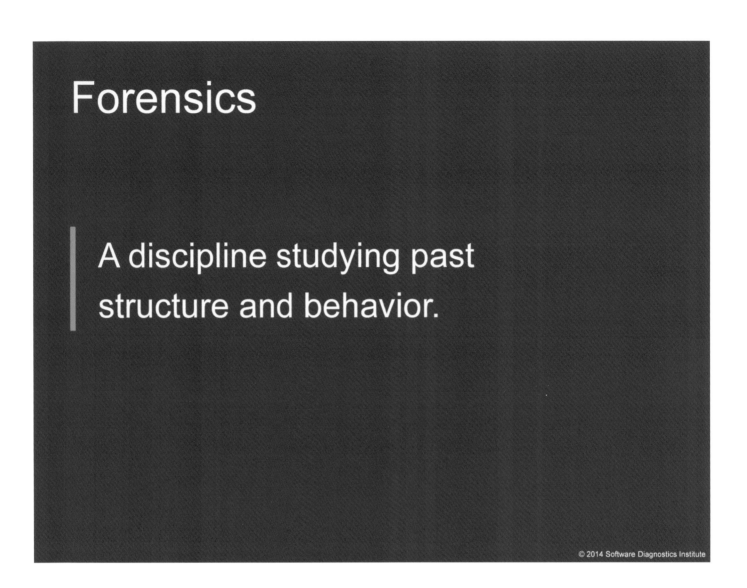

This is a typical definition of forensic science or forensics: a discipline studying past structure and behavior.

Memory Forensics

> A discipline studying past structure and behavior in acquired computer memory.

© 2014 Software Diagnostics Institute

There are many specialized forensics. Our concern is with memory forensics - investigation of past software structure behaviour in memory snapshots.

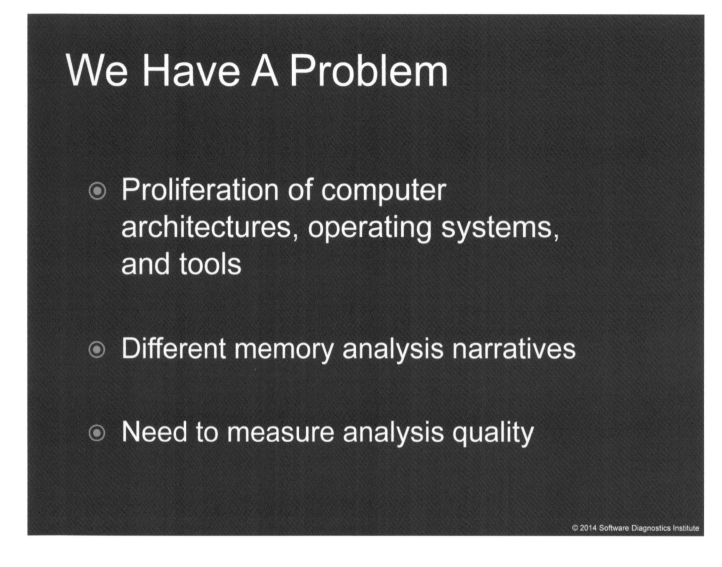

© 2014 Software Diagnostics Institute

However, we have a problem. There are so many different hardware and CPU architectures, operating systems, and even memory acquisition and analysis tools for the same hardware and software. If the same tool is used by different people we get different memory analysis reports where the same problems and incidents are retold differently. There is also the absence of quality measurements or if there are some measurements they are subjective at most.

Solution

⊙ **Empirical patterns**

⊙ **A pattern language**

⊙ **Pattern orientation**

© 2014 Software Diagnostics Institute

The solution to this problem is a unified language for discussing and communicating detection and analysis results. Such a language is usually called a pattern language. Empirically encountered patterns of detection and analysis are discerned and organized into pattern catalogues. This approach is very similar to software design patterns and was originally devised for town and building architecture by Christopher Alexander. We can paraphrase his book *"The Timeless Way of Building"* as *"The Timeless Way of Memory Forensics"*. By pattern orientation we mean the whole system of such patterns, their discovery, systematic usage, and life cycle.

Forensic Pattern

A common recurrent identifiable set of indicators (signs) together with a set of recommendations to apply in a specific context.

© 2014 Software Diagnostics Institute

Here we provide a definition of a general forensic pattern already put forward in our previous presentations: a common recurrent identifiable set of indicators (signs) together with a set of recommendations to apply in a specific context.

Memory Forensics revised

A discipline studying past structure and behavior of software in acquired memory using pattern-oriented analysis methodology.

© 2014 Software Diagnostics Institute

Now, we revise memory forensics definition taking into account the proposed pattern orientation.

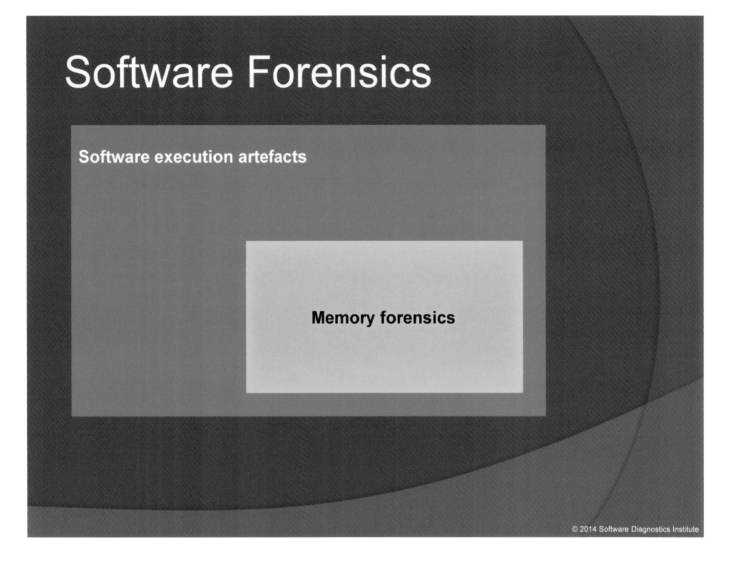

Memory forensics is a part of software forensics which considers many types of software execution artefacts and not only memory snapshots.

Software Forensics

A discipline studying past structure and behavior of software in execution artifacts using systemic and pattern-oriented analysis methodologies.

© 2014 Software Diagnostics Institute

This is a definition of software forensics we put forward in one of our previous presentations: a discipline studying past structure and behavior of software in execution artifacts using systemic and pattern-oriented analysis methodologies. Please notice the addition of the so called "systemic" approach. Although this is beyond the scope of this lecture we devoted one slide for it later on.

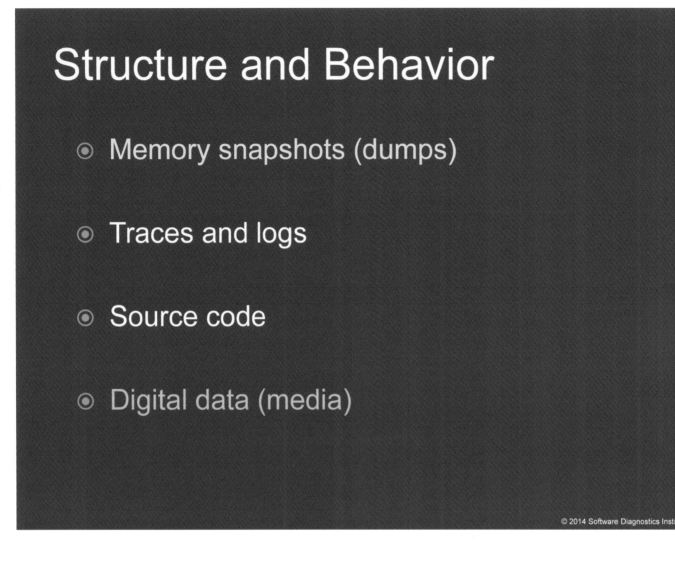

Structure and Behavior

- ◉ Memory snapshots (dumps)

- ◉ Traces and logs

- ◉ Source code

- ◉ Digital data (media)

© 2014 Software Diagnostics Institute

Here we provide the list of various software execution artefacts studied by software forensics. In memory forensics we are concerned mostly with memory dumps but the same approach and language can be applied to other digital data.

Diagnostics and Forensics

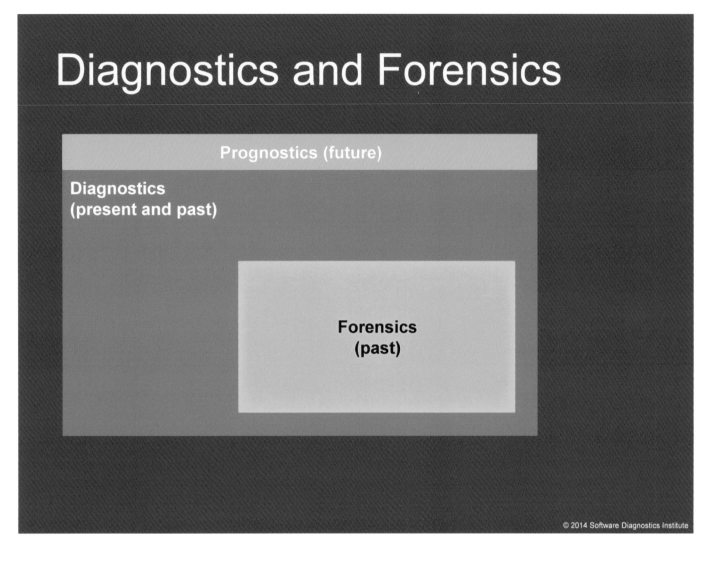

We also put software forensics and therefore memory forensics as a part of software diagnostics which analyses present and past of software execution.

Software Diagnostics

A discipline studying signs of software structure and behavior in software execution artifacts (such as memory dumps, software and network traces and logs) using systemic and pattern-oriented analysis methodologies.

© 2014 Software Diagnostics Institute

Here we provide a encompassing definition of software diagnostics: a discipline studying signs of software structure and behavior in software execution artifacts (such as memory dumps, software and network traces and logs) using systemic and pattern-oriented analysis methodologies.

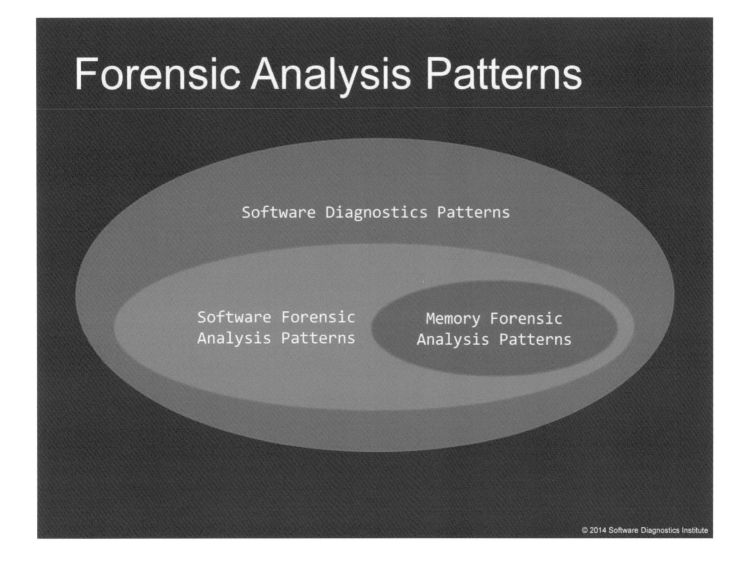

Naturally, because of that inclusion relationship, a set of memory forensic analysis patterns is a subset of software diagnostics patterns.

A Pattern Language

⊙ The same detection and analysis language for different computer architectures, operating systems, and tools

⊙ The same memory analysis narratives

⊙ Measured analysis quality

⊙ Predicting unknown

© 2014 Software Diagnostics Institute

Now having a pattern language we can state its benefits. Moreover, we can predict unknown software structure and behavior for a new computer platform by using the same pattern language from a more *"developed"* system. Here, by a more *developed* system we mean a system where the most patterns were discovered and elaborated. For example, we were able to do it for Mac OS X by reusing the same patterns from Windows, for ARM by reusing from x86/x64, and for GDB and LLDB by reusing WinDbg. We are now working on applying the same pattern language to Volatility.

Pattern Orientation

1. ## Pattern-driven

   - Finding patterns in memory
   - Using checklists and pattern catalogs

2. ## Pattern-based

   - Pattern catalogue evolution
   - Catalog packaging and delivery

© 2014 Software Diagnostics Institute

Now we'd like to say a few words about pattern orientation. We say it is pattern-driven when we talk about a forensic process and pattern recognition and a pattern-based when we talk about pattern life cycle. We start with the pattern-driven part first.

Main Pattern Catalogues

Memory Acquisition Patterns

Disassembly, Deconstruction, Reversing Patterns

Memory Analysis Patterns

...
Wait Chain
Execution Residue
Spiking Thread
Local Buffer Overflow
Shared Buffer Overwrite
Dynamic Memory
  Corruption
...

Malware Analysis Patterns

...
Raw Pointer
String Hint
Out-of-Module Pointer
Hooksware
Hidden Process
Deviant Module
Namespace
...

Structural Memory Patterns

...
Memory Region
Region Boundary
Anchor Region
Linked List
Value References
Regular Data
String Value
Small Value
Data Structure
...

© 2014 Software Diagnostics Institute

Patterns are organized into pattern catalogues. For memory forensics we are interested in 3 main ones such as memory analysis patterns, structural memory patterns and malware analysis patterns. These catalogues overlap because it is not easy sometimes to classify patterns rigidly. The basic motivation behind malware patterns is intentional abnormal software structure and behaviour whereas historically memory analysis patterns were collected for unintentional software behaviour arising from software defects with structural patterns added later but before the malware catalogue. In case of malware, rootkits, viruses, and in some complex cases of unintentional incidents a bit of disassembly and reversing may be required and we recently added a special pattern catalogue. Obviously, the timeless way of memory acquisition can be analysed and systematized in a pattern language terminology too. For the first 3 overlapping catalogues we provided a few pattern name examples and some of them will be shown in the practical part.

Pattern Classification

...

Dynamic Memory Corruption Patterns

Stack Overflow Patterns

Stack Trace Patterns

Symbol Patterns

Exception Patterns

Meta-Memory Dump Patterns

Module Patterns

Optimization Patterns

Thread Patterns

Process Patterns

...

© 2014 Software Diagnostics Institute

If a catalogue is too big it can be split into subcatalogues. For example, memory analysis catalogue contains almost 300 patterns and it was classified further. It is an ongoing process.

Memory Acquisition Patterns

http://www.dumpanalysis.org/memory-acquisition-patterns

Structural space patterns

...

Process Memory Dump
Kernel memory Dump
Physical Memory Dump
Fiber Bundle Dump

...

Acquisition strategy patterns

...

External Dump
Self Dump
Conditional Dump
Dump Sequence

...

© 2014 Software Diagnostics Institute

We also proposed a set of memory acquisition patterns and even split them into two groups based on what we dump, and why, how, and when we dump. Here we provide a few self-evident pattern name examples.

The current list of memory acquisition patterns:
http://www.dumpanalysis.org/memory-acquisition-patterns

ADDR Patterns

http://www.dumpanalysis.org/addr-patterns

...

Potential Functionality	Memory Copy
Function Skeleton	Call Prologue
Function Call	Call Parameter
Call Path	Call Epilogue
Local Variable	Call Result
Static Variable	Control Path
Pointer Dereference	Function Parameter
Function Prologue	Structure Field
Function Epilogue	Last Call
Variable Initialization	...

© 2014 Software Diagnostics Institute

These are typical patterns we call ADDR. The complete description will be available in the forthcoming volume 8 of Memory Dump Analysis Anthology. The name ADDR is based on the name if the course Accelerated Disassembly, Deconstruction, and Reversing where they were first introduced.

The current list of ADDR patterns:

http://www.dumpanalysis.org/addr-patterns

Pattern Implementation

- By OS vendor (Windows, Mac OS X, Linux, …)

- By tool (WinDbg, Volatility, IDA, GDB, LLDB, …)

- By CPU architecture (x86, x64, ARM, …)

- By digital media (memory, volume, file, blob, …)

© 2014 Software Diagnostics Institute

Ultimately patterns are found on specific platforms. By pattern implementation we mean differences in operating systems, product lines, media types, CPU and hardware architectures. The same name may share different implementations.

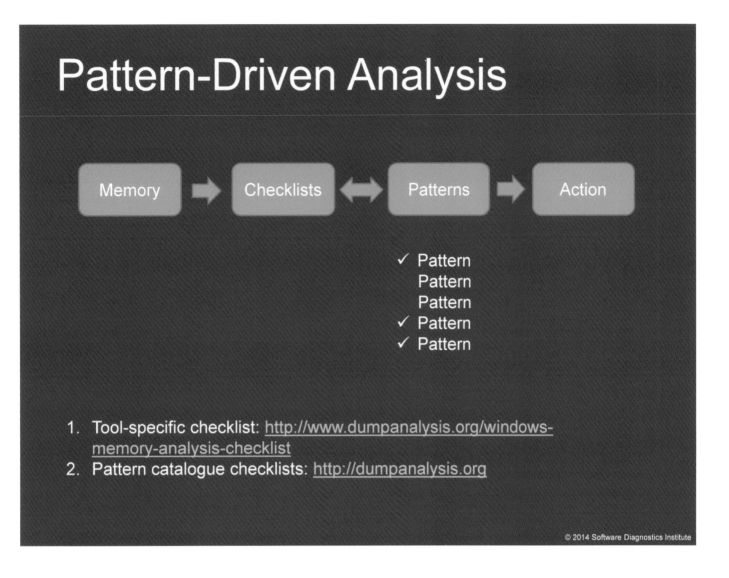

Now we'd like to say a few words about checklists. This is an essential feature of pattern-driven software diagnostics and therefore memory forensics. There are 2 types of checklists. A tool specific checklist may be the list of commands and recommendations. More general pattern catalogue checklist provides the list of patterns to check for.

Tool-specific checklist:

http://www.dumpanalysis.org/windows-memory-analysis-checklist

Pattern catalogue checklists:

http://dumpanalysis.org

Pattern-Based Analysis

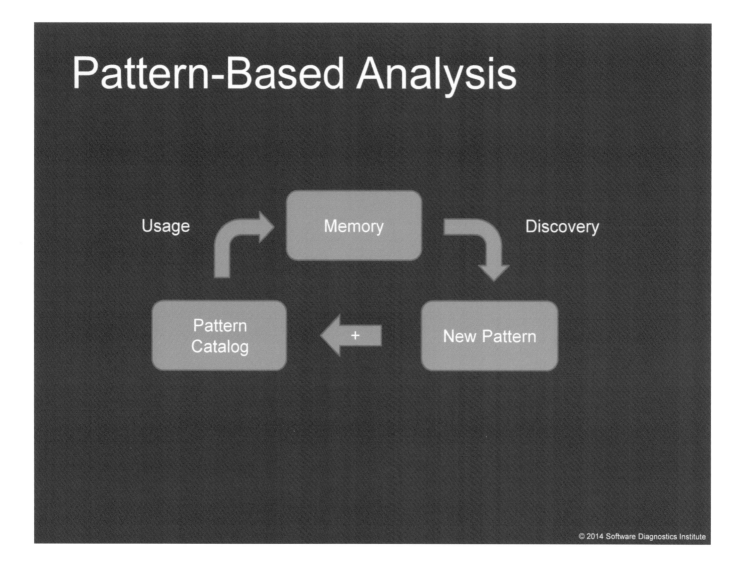

© 2014 Software Diagnostics Institute

Pattern catalogs are rarely fixed. New patterns are constantly discerned, refined, and reclassified. This is the essence of the pattern-based part of pattern orientation.

Systems Approach

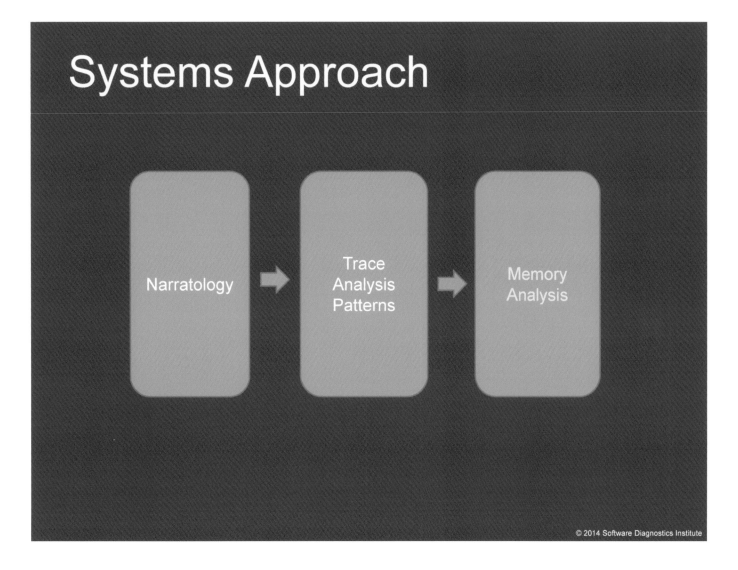

© 2014 Software Diagnostics Institute

At the end of this theoretical part we provide a few words about the systems approach mentioned earlier. This is an application of ideas and methods from different disciplines. For example, narratology, a study of narratives such as novels and stories, was applied to trace and log analysis. The result was a trace analysis pattern catalogue which can also be applied to memory analysis and even to analysis process itself. We list a reference to Systemic Software Diagnostics at the end of this presentation.

Native Memory Forensics

Using native OS debuggers such as WinDbg from Debugging Tools for Windows or GDB (Linux) or GDB/LLDB (Mac OS X).

© 2014 Software Diagnostics Institute

We'd like to make a note before the practical part. Among different tools for memory forensic analysis native OS debuggers can be used. We use one of them here to illustrate the pattern language.

Practical Examples

WinDbg session…

© 2014 Software Diagnostics Institute

Patterns for Example A

- Tampered Dump
- Exception Stack Trace
- Stored Exception
- Lateral Damage
- Execution Residue
- Hidden Exception
- NULL Data Pointer

© 2014 Software Diagnostics Institute

*This example is adapted with some modifications from **Tampered Dump** pattern description published in Software Diagnostics Library.*

The availability of direct dump modification raises the possibility of **Tampered Dumps**. These are memory dumps specifically modified to alter structural and behavioral diagnostic patterns, for example, to suppress certain module involvement or introduce fictitious past objects and interaction traces. There can be 2 types of such artefacts: strong tampering with new or altered information completely integrated into memory fabric and weak tampering to confuse inexperienced software support engineers and memory forensics analysts.

In this exercise we look at one such experimental process memory dump made from the previously crashed Windows Calculator, calc.exe.

After we open the dump we fix symbols, set up a log file to record all command output, and list loaded modules:

```
0:003> .symfix c:\mss

0:003> .reload

0:003> .logopen C:\MemoryDumps\tampered.log
Opened log file ' C:\MemoryDumps\tampered.log'

0:003> lm
start             end               module name
00000000`76ea0000 00000000`76fbf000  kernel32    (deferred)
00000000`76fc0000 00000000`770ba000  user32      (deferred)
00000000`770c0000 00000000`77269000  ntdll       (pdb symbols)
c:\mss\ntdll.pdb\9D04EB0AA387494FBD81ED062072B99C2\ntdll.pdb
00000000`ffd90000 00000000`ffe73000  calc        (deferred)
000007fe`f5c00000 000007fe`f5c54000  oleacc      (deferred)
000007fe`f6850000 000007fe`f6a66000  GdiPlus     (deferred)
000007fe`f9c10000 000007fe`f9c4b000  winmm       (deferred)
000007fe`fae80000 000007fe`fafe1000  WindowsCodecs   (deferred)
000007fe`fb1d0000 000007fe`fb1e8000  dwmapi      (deferred)
000007fe`fb600000 000007fe`fb656000  uxtheme     (deferred)
000007fe`fb7e0000 000007fe`fb9d4000  comctl32    (deferred)
000007fe`fbf90000 000007fe`fbf9c000  version     (deferred)
000007fe`fcdb0000 000007fe`fcdbf000  CRYPTBASE   (deferred)
000007fe`fd060000 000007fe`fd0cb000  KERNELBASE   (pdb symbols)
c:\mss\kernelbase.pdb\88D04DC8E39B4CBB9CB12366C2AE475F2\kernelbase.pdb
000007fe`fd2b0000 000007fe`fd34f000  msvcrt      (deferred)
000007fe`fd350000 000007fe`fd42b000  advapi32    (deferred)
000007fe`fd430000 000007fe`fd45e000  imm32       (deferred)
000007fe`fd460000 000007fe`fd47f000  sechost     (deferred)
000007fe`fd480000 000007fe`fd683000  ole32       (deferred)
000007fe`fd690000 000007fe`fd729000  clbcatq     (deferred)
000007fe`fd7b0000 000007fe`fd7be000  lpk         (deferred)
000007fe`fdc00000 000007fe`fdcc9000  usp10       (deferred)
000007fe`fdcd0000 000007fe`fea58000  shell32     (deferred)
000007fe`fef60000 000007fe`fefc7000  gdi32       (deferred)
000007fe`fefd0000 000007fe`ff0a7000  oleaut32    (deferred)
000007fe`ff0b0000 000007fe`ff1dd000  rpcrt4      (deferred)
000007fe`ff240000 000007fe`ff2b1000  shlwapi     (deferred)
000007fe`ff2c0000 000007fe`ff3c9000  msctf       (deferred)
```

We see **Exception Stack Trace** pointing to a problem in *calc* module:

```
0:003> k
Child-SP RetAddr Call Site
00000000`0244e858 000007fe`fd061430 ntdll!NtWaitForMultipleObjects+0xa
00000000`0244e860 00000000`76ec1723 KERNELBASE!WaitForMultipleObjectsEx+0xe8
00000000`0244e960 00000000`76f3b5e5 kernel32!WaitForMultipleObjectsExImplementation+0xb3
00000000`0244e9f0 00000000`76f3b767 kernel32!WerpReportFaultInternal+0x215
00000000`0244ea90 00000000`76f3b7bf kernel32!WerpReportFault+0x77
00000000`0244eac0 00000000`76f3b9dc kernel32!BasepReportFault+0x1f
00000000`0244eaf0 00000000`77153398 kernel32!UnhandledExceptionFilter+0x1fc
00000000`0244ebd0 00000000`770d85c8 ntdll! ?? ::FNODOBFM::`string'+0x2365
00000000`0244ec00 00000000`770e9d2d ntdll!_C_specific_handler+0x8c
00000000`0244ec70 00000000`770d91cf ntdll!RtlpExecuteHandlerForException+0xd
00000000`0244eca0 00000000`77111248 ntdll!RtlDispatchException+0x45a
00000000`0244f380 00000000`ffdbdb27 ntdll!KiUserExceptionDispatch+0x2e
00000000`0244fab0 00000000`76eb59ed calc!CTimedCalc::WatchDogThread+0xb2
00000000`0244faf0 00000000`770ec541 kernel32!BaseThreadInitThunk+0xd
00000000`0244fb20 00000000`00000000 ntdll!RtlUserThreadStart+0x1d
```

The default analysis command (**!analyse -v**) diagnoses *"stack corruption"*:

```
FAULTING_IP:
kernel32!UnhandledExceptionFilter+1fc
00000000`76f3b9dc 448bf0 mov r14d,eax


EXCEPTION_RECORD: ffffffffffffffff -- (.exr 0xffffffffffffffff)
ExceptionAddress: 0000000076f3b9dc (kernel32!UnhandledExceptionFilter+0x00000000000001fc)
ExceptionCode: 0244e9f0
ExceptionFlags: 00000000
NumberParameters: 0


DEFAULT_BUCKET_ID: STACK_CORRUPTION


PRIMARY_PROBLEM_CLASS: STACK_CORRUPTION


BUGCHECK_STR: APPLICATION_FAULT_STACK_CORRUPTION


IP_ON_HEAP: 8d483674c33bfffa
The fault address in not in any loaded module, please check your build's rebase
log at <releasedir>\bin\build_logs\timebuild\ntrebase.log for module which may
contain the address if it were loaded.


UNALIGNED_STACK_POINTER: 0000000076f3b767


STACK_TEXT:
00000000`00000000 00000000`00000000 calc!CTimedCalc::WatchDogThread+0x0


FOLLOWUP_IP:
calc!CTimedCalc::WatchDogThread+0
00000000`ffd92254 48895c2408 mov qword ptr [rsp+8],rbx
```

Stored Exception resembles signs of **Local Buffer Overflow** (but segment register values and CPU flags have suspiciously invalid values, possibly **Lateral Damage**):

```
0:003> .ecxr
rax=0000000000000000 rbx=0000000000000001 rcx=000000000244ec30
rdx=000000000244ec30 rsi=0100000000000080 rdi=0000000000000158
rip=0000000076f3b9dc rsp=0000000076f3b767 rbp=0000000000000000
r8=0000000000000000 r9=ffffffffffffffff r10=0000000076f3b7bf
r11=000000000244ec30 r12=0000000000000001 r13=0000000000000000
r14=0000000000000000 r15=0000000000000000
iopl=0         nv up di pl nz na pe nc
cs=0000 ss=0000 ds=0266 es=0000 fs=0000 gs=0154 efl=00000000
kernel32!UnhandledExceptionFilter+0×1fc:
00000000`76f3b9dc 448bf0 mov r14d,eax


0:003> k
*** Stack trace for last set context - .thread/.cxr resets it
Child-SP RetAddr Call Site
00000000`76f3b767 8d483674`c33bfffa kernel32!UnhandledExceptionFilter+0x1fc
00000000`76f3b847 5aa3e800`05bfac0d 0x8d483674`c33bfffa
00000000`76f3b84f ebffcf83`48ccfff9 0x5aa3e800`05bfac0d
00000000`76f3b857 8348c000`0409ba27 0xebffcf83`48ccfff9
00000000`76f3b85f 54dfe8cf`8b48ffcf 0x8348c000`0409ba27
00000000`76f3b867 4c02778d`db33fff9 0x54dfe8cf`8b48ffcf
00000000`76f3b86f 4c000000`e024a48b 0x4c02778d`db33fff9
00000000`76f3b877 ffcf8348`04ebeb8b 0x4c000000`e024a48b
00000000`76f3b87f fffc59e9`e8cc8b49 0xffcf8348`04ebeb8b
00000000`76f3b887 42e9c78b`0775c73b 0xfffc59e9`e8cc8b49
00000000`76f3b88f fffa6fa9`e8000003 0x42e9c78b`0775c73b
00000000`76f3b897 32e9c033`0774c33b 0xfffa6fa9`e8000003
00000000`76f3b89f fa7f3d8d`4c000003 0x32e9c033`0774c33b
00000000`76f3b8a7 de15ffcf`8b490006 0xfa7f3d8d`4c000003
00000000`76f3b8af f9370d8b`4800000e 0xde15ffcf`8b490006
00000000`76f3b8b7 000014a1`15ff0006 0xf9370d8b`4800000e
00000000`76f3b8bf 840fc33b`48f08b4c 0x000014a1`15ff0006
00000000`76f3b8c7 f6158b48`00000099 0x840fc33b`48f08b4c
00000000`76f3b8cf 0238c281`480006f3 0xf6158b48`00000099
00000000`76f3b8d7 48cfe8c8`8b480000 0x0238c281`480006f3
00000000`76f3b8df 8b4c7f74`c33bfff9 0x48cfe8c8`8b480000
00000000`76f3b8e7 888b4900`06f3dc05 0x8b4c7f74`c33bfff9
00000000`76f3b8ef 75083949`00000238 0x888b4900`06f3dc05
00000000`76f3b8f7 00000240`808b496c 0x75083949`00000238
00000000`76f3b8ff 8b415f75`08403949 0x00000240`808b496c
00000000`76f3b907 00024880`3b411040 0x8b415f75`08403949
00000000`76f3b90f 01040000`a9527500 0x00024880`3b411040
00000000`76f3b917 00025090`8d491874 0x01040000`a9527500
00000000`76f3b91f c68a4418`488d4900 0x00025090`8d491874
00000000`76f3b927 c33a0000`117315ff 0xc68a4418`488d4900
00000000`76f3b92f 4e15ffcf`8b493374 0xc33a0000`117315ff
00000000`76f3b937 ff41cc8b`4900000e 0x4e15ffcf`8b493374
00000000`76f3b93f 00028c84`0fc63bd6 0xff41cc8b`4900000e
00000000`76f3b947 00028484`0fc73b00 0x00028c84`0fc63bd6
00000000`76f3b94f 6ee7e819`75c33b00 0x00028484`0fc73b00
00000000`76f3b957 c0331074`c33bfffa 0x6ee7e819`75c33b00
00000000`76f3b95f cf8b4900`000270e9 0xc0331074`c33bfffa
00000000`76f3b967 8b490000`0e1b15ff 0xcf8b4900`000270e9
00000000`76f3b96f 3b000013`e215ffcc 0x8b490000`0e1b15ff
00000000`76f3b977 0253e9c7`8b0775c7 0x3b000013`e215ffcc
00000000`76f3b97f 41fff959`4ae80000 0x0253e9c7`8b0775c7
00000000`76f3b987 c6844100`000002be 0x41fff959`4ae80000
```

```
00000000`76f3b98f 15ff0000`023d850f 0xc6844100`000002be
00000000`76f3b997 850f20a8`00000f65 0x15ff0000`023d850f
00000000`76f3b99f 245c8948`0000022f 0x850f20a8`00000f65
00000000`76f3b9a7 448d4c3e`4e8d4520 0x245c8948`0000022f
00000000`76f3b9af ffc933d6`8b416024 0x448d4c3e`4e8d4520
00000000`76f3b9b7 7cc33b00`0009f415 0xffc933d6`8b416024
00000000`76f3b9bf 730a7024`64ba0f0f 0x7cc33b00`0009f415
00000000`76f3b9c7 00000205`e9c68b07 0x730a7024`64ba0f0f
00000000`76f3b9cf cc8b49d6`8bfb8b44 0x00000205`e9c68b07
00000000`76f3b9d7 f08b44ff`fffdc4e8 0xcc8b49d6`8bfb8b44
00000000`76f3b9df e9c03307`7508f883 0xf08b44ff`fffdc4e8
00000000`76f3b9e7 7506f883`000001e9 0xe9c03307`7508f883
00000000`76f3b9ef c33bfffa`6e4be810 0x7506f883`000001e9
00000000`76f3b9f7 0001d4e9`c0330774 0xc33bfffa`6e4be810
00000000`76f3b9ff 86850f04`fe834100 0x0001d4e9`c0330774
00000000`76f3ba07 0000024a`ba000001 0x86850f04`fe834100
00000000`76f3ba0f 00b841ce`8b45c933 0x0000024a`ba000001
00000000`76f3ba17 fff7a249`e8000010 0x00b841ce`8b45c933
00000000`76f3ba1f 0775c33b`48e88b4c 0xfff7a249`e8000010
00000000`76f3ba27 48000001`a6e9c033 0x0775c33b`48e88b4c
00000000`76f3ba2f 24448948`3024448d 0x48000001`a6e9c033
00000000`76f3ba37 0000f024`8c8d4c20 0x24448948`3024448d
00000000`76f3ba3f 49000001`25b84100 0x0000f024`8c8d4c20
00000000`76f3ba47 8a0fe8cf`8b48d58b 0x49000001`25b84100
00000000`76f3ba4f 4166097c`c33bfffe 0x8a0fe8cf`8b48d58b
00000000`76f3ba57 39fe450f`44005d39 0x4166097c`c33bfffe
00000000`76f3ba5f 850f0000`00f0249c 0x39fe450f`44005d39
00000000`76f3ba67 240c8b49`000000bc 0x850f0000`00f0249c
00000000`76f3ba6f 40244489`48016348 0x240c8b49`000000bc
00000000`76f3ba77 24448948`10418b48 0x40244489`48016348
00000000`76f3ba7f 75c00000`06398148 0x24448948`10418b48
00000000`76f3ba87 480b7203`18798318 0x75c00000`06398148
00000000`76f3ba8f 50244489`4830418b 0x480b7203`18798318
00000000`76f3ba97 eb50245c`89481ceb 0x50244489`4830418b
00000000`76f3ba9f 8b480b72`18713915 0xeb50245c`89481ceb
00000000`76f3baa7 eb502444`89482041 0x8b480b72`18713915
00000000`76f3baaf 02ba5024`5c894805 0xeb502444`89482041
00000000`76f3bab7 0b721851`39000000 0x02ba5024`5c894805
00000000`76f3babf 24448948`28418b48 0x0b721851`39000000
00000000`76f3bac7 58245c89`4805eb58 0x24448948`28418b48
00000000`76f3bacf ba1d3808`74fb3b44 0x58245c89`4805eb58
00000000`76f3bad7 48d68b02`740006fd 0xba1d3808`74fb3b44
00000000`76f3badf 48000000`e824848d 0x48d68b02`740006fd
00000000`76f3bae7 20245489`28244489 0x48000000`e824848d
00000000`76f3baef c0334540`244c8d4c 0x20245489`28244489
00000000`76f3baf7 000144b9`04508d41 0xc0334540`244c8d4c
00000000`76f3baff ba00000d`7215ffd0 0x000144b9`04508d41
00000000`76f3bb07 8c8bc223`c0000000 0xba00000d`7215ffd0
00000000`76f3bb0f b8c23b00`0000e824 0x8c8bc223`c0000000
00000000`76f3bb17 89c8440f`00000006 0xb8c23b00`0000e824
00000000`76f3bb1f 07eb0000`00e8248c 0x89c8440f`00000006
00000000`76f3bb27 44000000`e8248c8b 0x07eb0000`00e8248c
00000000`76f3bb2f 7403f983`5d74fb3b 0x44000000`e8248c8b
00000000`76f3bb37 000000f0`249c3909 0x7403f983`5d74fb3b
00000000`76f3bb3f 0006fd4d`058a4f74 0x000000f0`249c3909
00000000`76f3bb47 f85f5ce8`4b75c33a 0x0006fd4d`058a4f74
00000000`76f3bb4f 448b3b75`5c5838ff 0xf85f5ce8`4b75c33a
00000000`76f3bb57 894c2824`44893024 0x448b3b75`5c5838ff
00000000`76f3bb5f 08244c8b`4d20246c 0x894c2824`44893024
00000000`76f3bb67 fec2c748`24048b4d 0x08244c8b`4d20246c
```

```
00000000`76f3bb6f  b6e8cf8b`48ffffff  0xfec2c748`24048b4d
00000000`76f3bb77  fd130db6`0fffffea  0xb6e8cf8b`48ffffff
00000000`76f3bb7f  88ce4c0f`c33b0006  0xfd130db6`0fffffea
00000000`76f3bb87  ebfb8b00`06fd080d  0x88ce4c0f`c33b0006
00000000`76f3bb8f  3a0006fc`fe058a29  0xebfb8b00`06fd080d
00000000`76f3bb97  8b240c8b`491874c3  0x3a0006fc`fe058a29
00000000`76f3bb9f  060f15ff`cf8b4811  0x8b240c8b`491874c3
00000000`76f3bba7  0000f824`bc8b0000  0x060f15ff`cf8b4811
00000000`76f3bbaf  00f824bc`8b07eb00  0x0000f824`bc8b0000
00000000`76f3bbb7  331074eb`3b4c0000  0x00f824bc`8b07eb00
00000000`76f3bbbf  49000080`00b841d2  0x331074eb`3b4c0000
00000000`76f3bbc7  8bfff74b`5ae8cd8b  0x49000080`00b841d2
00000000`76f3bbcf  c48148c6`8b02ebc7  0x8bfff74b`5ae8cd8b
00000000`76f3bbd7  5e415f41`000000a0  0xc48148c6`8b02ebc7
00000000`76f3bbdf  c35b5e5f`5c415d41  0x5e415f41`000000a0
00000000`76f3bbe7  158ead00`00000090  0xc35b5e5f`5c415d41
00000000`76f3bbef  00000200`00000053  0x158ead00`00000090
00000000`76f3bbf7  09bc2400`00002500  0x00000200`00000053
00000000`76f3bbff  00000000`09b42400  0x09bc2400`00002500
00000000`76f3bc07  7e023553`158ead00  0x9b42400
00000000`76f3bc0f  00000400`00000a19  0x7e023553`158ead00
00000000`76f3bc17  09b42000`09bc2000  0x00000400`00000a19
00000000`76f3bc1f  445352bb`03197e00  0x09b42000`09bc2000
00000000`76f3bc27  4c886225`48e28953  0x445352bb`03197e00
00000000`76f3bc2f  4fb29af4`dfbb8344  0x4c886225`48e28953
00000000`76f3bc37  72656b00`0000020e  0x4fb29af4`dfbb8344
00000000`76f3bc3f  64702e32`336c656e  0x72656b00`0000020e
00000000`76f3bc47  00000000`00000062  0x64702e32`336c656e
```

We check for any **Hidden Exceptions** among **Execution Residue** and find it was **NULL Data Pointer**:

```
0:003> .cxr
Resetting default scope

0:003> k
Child-SP          RetAddr          Call Site
00000000`0244e858 000007fe`fd061430 ntdll!NtWaitForMultipleObjects+0xa
00000000`0244e860 00000000`76ec1723 KERNELBASE!WaitForMultipleObjectsEx+0xe8
00000000`0244e960 00000000`76f3b5e5 kernel32!WaitForMultipleObjectsExImplementation+0xb3
00000000`0244e9f0 00000000`76f3b767 kernel32!WerpReportFaultInternal+0x215
00000000`0244ea90 00000000`76f3b7bf kernel32!WerpReportFault+0x77
00000000`0244eac0 00000000`76f3b9dc kernel32!BasepReportFault+0x1f
00000000`0244eaf0 00000000`77153398 kernel32!UnhandledExceptionFilter+0x1fc
00000000`0244ebd0 00000000`770d85c8 ntdll! ?? ::FNODOBFM::`string'+0x2365
00000000`0244ec00 00000000`770e9d2d ntdll!_C_specific_handler+0x8c
00000000`0244ec70 00000000`770d91cf ntdll!RtlpExecuteHandlerForException+0xd
00000000`0244eca0 00000000`77111248 ntdll!RtlDispatchException+0x45a
00000000`0244f380 00000000`ffdbdb27 ntdll!KiUserExceptionDispatch+0x2e
00000000`0244fab0 00000000`76eb59ed calc!CTimedCalc::WatchDogThread+0xb2
00000000`0244faf0 00000000`770ec541 kernel32!BaseThreadInitThunk+0xd
00000000`0244fb20 00000000`00000000 ntdll!RtlUserThreadStart+0x1d
```

```
0:003> dps 00000000`0244eca0 00000000`0244fab0
00000000`0244eca0  00000000`02450000
00000000`0244eca8  00000000`76fadda0 kernel32!__PchSym_ <PERF> (kernel32+0x10dda0)
00000000`0244ecb0  00000000`00012f00
00000000`0244ecb8  00000000`7711920a ntdll!RtlDosApplyFileIsolationRedirection_Ustr+0x3da
00000000`0244ecc0  00000000`00000005
00000000`0244ecc8  00000000`00000000
00000000`0244ecd0  00000000`00000000
00000000`0244ecd8  00000000`00000000
00000000`0244ece0  00000000`0244fb20
00000000`0244ece8  00000000`00000000
00000000`0244ecf0  00000000`77202dd0 ntdll!CsrPortMemoryRemoteDelta <PERF> (ntdll+0x142dd0)
00000000`0244ecf8  00000000`00000000
00000000`0244ed00  00000000`00000000
00000000`0244ed08  00000000`02450000
00000000`0244ed10  00000000`771e8180 ntdll!`string'+0xc040
00000000`0244ed18  00000000`0244b000
00000000`0244ed20  00000000`0244f250
00000000`0244ed28  00000000`770c0000 ntdll!RtlDeactivateActivationContext <PERF> (ntdll+0x0)
00000000`0244ed30  00000000`770ec541 ntdll!RtlUserThreadStart+0x1d
00000000`0244ed38  00000000`770c0000 ntdll!RtlDeactivateActivationContext <PERF> (ntdll+0x0)
00000000`0244ed40  00000000`77202dd0 ntdll!CsrPortMemoryRemoteDelta <PERF> (ntdll+0x142dd0)
00000000`0244ed48  00000000`0244fb20
00000000`0244ed50  00000000`771d7718 ntdll!LdrpDefaultExtension
00000000`0244ed58  00000000`0244ed80
00000000`0244ed60  00000000`770d852c ntdll!_C_specific_handler
00000000`0244ed68  00000000`771e8180 ntdll!`string'+0xc040
00000000`0244ed70  00000000`0244f250
00000000`0244ed78  00000000`00000000
00000000`0244ed80  00000000`00000000
00000000`0244ed88  00000000`00000000
00000000`0244ed90  00000000`00000000
00000000`0244ed98  00000000`00000000
00000000`0244eda0  00000000`00000000
00000000`0244eda8  00000000`00000000
00000000`0244edb0  00001f80`00000000
00000000`0244edb8  00000000`00000033
00000000`0244edc0  00010246`002b0000
00000000`0244edc8  00000000`00000000
00000000`0244edd0  00000000`00000000
00000000`0244edd8  00000000`00000000
00000000`0244ede0  00000000`00000000
00000000`0244ede8  000007fe`ff3625c0 msctf!s_szCompClassName
00000000`0244edf0  00000000`00200000
00000000`0244edf8  00000000`0244ee40
00000000`0244ee00  00000000`0244ee40
00000000`0244ee08  00000000`0244ee40
00000000`0244ee10  00000000`00000000
00000000`0244ee18  00000000`0244fb70
00000000`0244ee20  00000000`00000000
00000000`0244ee28  00000000`00000000
00000000`0244ee30  00000000`00000000
00000000`0244ee38  000007fe`fd602790 ole32!`string'
00000000`0244ee40  00000000`00292170
00000000`0244ee48  00000000`770e7a33 ntdll!LdrpFindOrMapDll+0x138
00000000`0244ee50  00000000`0244ef68
00000000`0244ee58  00000000`00000000
00000000`0244ee60  00000000`00000000
00000000`0244ee68  00000000`00000000
00000000`0244ee70  00000000`00000000
```

```
00000000`0244ee78 00000000`00000000
00000000`0244ee80 00000000`0000027f
00000000`0244ee88 00000000`00000000
00000000`0244ee90 00000000`00000000
00000000`0244ee98 0000ffff`00001f80
00000000`0244eea0 00000000`00000000
00000000`0244eea8 00000000`00000000
00000000`0244eeb0 00000000`00000000
00000000`0244eeb8 00000000`00000000
00000000`0244eec0 00000000`00000000
00000000`0244eec8 00000000`00000000
00000000`0244eed0 00000000`00000000
00000000`0244eed8 00000000`00000000
00000000`0244eee0 00000000`00000000
00000000`0244eee8 00000000`00000000
00000000`0244eef0 00000000`00000000
00000000`0244eef8 00000000`00000000
00000000`0244ef00 00000000`00000000
00000000`0244ef08 00000000`00000000
00000000`0244ef10 00000000`00000000
00000000`0244ef18 00000000`00000000
00000000`0244ef20 00000000`00000000
00000000`0244ef28 00000000`771192a8 ntdll!LdrpApplyFileNameRedirection+0x2d3
00000000`0244ef30 00000000`00000000
00000000`0244ef38 00000000`00000000
00000000`0244ef40 00000000`00000000
00000000`0244ef48 00000000`02080000
00000000`0244ef50 00000000`0244f028
00000000`0244ef58 00000000`0244f020
00000000`0244ef60 00000000`00000000
00000000`0244ef68 00000000`00000000
00000000`0244ef70 00000000`00000000
00000000`0244ef78 000007fe`fd602848 ole32!`string'
00000000`0244ef80 00000000`00000000
00000000`0244ef88 00000000`00000000
00000000`0244ef90 00000000`00000000
00000000`0244ef98 00000000`00000000
00000000`0244efa0 00000000`00000000
00000000`0244efa8 00000000`00000000
00000000`0244efb0 00000000`00000000
00000000`0244efb8 00000000`00000000
00000000`0244efc0 00000000`00000000
00000000`0244efc8 00000000`00000000
00000000`0244efd0 00000000`00000000
00000000`0244efd8 00000000`00000000
00000000`0244efe0 00000000`00000000
00000000`0244efe8 00000000`00000000
00000000`0244eff0 00000000`00000000
00000000`0244eff8 00000000`00000000
00000000`0244f000 00000000`00000000
00000000`0244f008 00000000`00000000
00000000`0244f010 00000000`00000000
00000000`0244f018 00000000`00000000
00000000`0244f020 00000000`0244f038
00000000`0244f028 00000000`0000011b
00000000`0244f030 00000000`024d0000
00000000`0244f038 00000080`001a024d
00000000`0244f040 00000000`01c0c8a0
00000000`0244f048 00000000`002f0101
00000000`0244f050 00000000`00000000
```

```
00000000`0244f058 00000000`00000022
00000000`0244f060 00000000`002f9b00
00000000`0244f068 00000000`01bd5390
00000000`0244f070 00000000`002f7c00
00000000`0244f078 00000000`01bd5580
00000000`0244f080 00000000`01bd57b0
00000000`0244f088 00000000`002f9b00
00000000`0244f090 00000000`00000000
00000000`0244f098 00000024`00000003
00000000`0244f0a0 00000000`002e91b0
00000000`0244f0a8 00000000`00000022
00000000`0244f0b0 00000000`771d5430 ntdll!RtlpInterceptorRoutines
00000000`0244f0b8 00000000`00000000
00000000`0244f0c0 00000000`00000010
00000000`0244f0c8 00000000`01bd0000
00000000`0244f0d0 00000000`00000008
00000000`0244f0d8 00000000`00000001
00000000`0244f0e0 00000000`01bd0288
00000000`0244f0e8 00000000`77113448 ntdll!RtlAllocateHeap+0xe4
00000000`0244f0f0 00000000`00000000
00000000`0244f0f8 00000000`00000001
00000000`0244f100 000002b2`000f002f
00000000`0244f108 00000000`01bd5780
00000000`0244f110 00000000`00250230
00000000`0244f118 00000000`000000df
00000000`0244f120 00000000`002551a0
00000000`0244f128 00000000`00255210
00000000`0244f130 00000000`002f9b00
00000000`0244f138 00000000`002551a0
00000000`0244f140 00000000`000000df
00000000`0244f148 00000000`10000010
00000000`0244f150 00000000`00250230
00000000`0244f158 00000000`00000000
00000000`0244f160 00000000`00250498
00000000`0244f168 00000000`0025026c
00000000`0244f170 00000000`002f9b00
00000000`0244f178 00000000`002551a0
00000000`0244f180 00000000`00000022
00000000`0244f188 00000000`76fd88b8 user32!GetPropW+0x4d
00000000`0244f190 00000000`00002974
00000000`0244f198 00000000`76fd88b8 user32!GetPropW+0x4d
00000000`0244f1a0 00000000`00250230
00000000`0244f1a8 00000000`76fd7931 user32!IsWindow+0x9
00000000`0244f1b0 00000000`002ed6d0
00000000`0244f1b8 00000000`76fd7931 user32!IsWindow+0x9
00000000`0244f1c0 00000000`00000000
00000000`0244f1c8 00000000`01c0c8d0
00000000`0244f1d0 00000000`01c0c8a0
00000000`0244f1d8 00000000`00000000
00000000`0244f1e0 00000000`00000008
00000000`0244f1e8 00000000`01bd0000
00000000`0244f1f0 00000000`00000000
00000000`0244f1f8 00000000`770f41c8 ntdll!RtlpReAllocateHeap+0x178
00000000`0244f200 00000000`00000002
00000000`0244f208 00000000`00000002
00000000`0244f210 00000000`00000000
00000000`0244f218 000007fe`4f00024d
00000000`0244f220 00000000`00000000
00000000`0244f228 000007fe`fb601381 uxtheme!CThemeWnd::_PreDefWindowProc+0x31
00000000`0244f230 00000000`00000082
```

```
00000000`0244f238  00000000`00000000
00000000`0244f240  00000000`7a337100
00000000`0244f248  00000000`01c0c8c0
00000000`0244f250  00000000`00000003
00000000`0244f258  00000000`76eb59e0  kernel32!BaseThreadInitThunk
00000000`0244f260  00000000`ffdbdb32  calc!CTimedCalc::Start+0xa9
00000000`0244f268  00000000`ffd90000  calc!CCalculatorController::CCalculatorController <PERF>
(calc+0x0)
00000000`0244f270  00000000`ffe0ac64  calc!_dyn_tls_init_callback <PERF> (calc+0x7ac64)
00000000`0244f278  00000000`76ea0000  kernel32!TestResourceDataMatchEntry <PERF> (kernel32+0x0)
00000000`0244f280  00000000`76fadda0  kernel32!__PchSym_ <PERF> (kernel32+0x10dda0)
00000000`0244f288  00000000`770c0000  ntdll!RtlDeactivateActivationContext <PERF> (ntdll+0x0)
00000000`0244f290  00000000`77202dd0  ntdll!CsrPortMemoryRemoteDelta <PERF> (ntdll+0x142dd0)
00000000`0244f298  00000000`76fd760e  user32!RealDefWindowProcW+0x5a
00000000`0244f2a0  00000000`00000001
00000000`0244f2a8  000007fe`fb600037  uxtheme!operator delete <PERF> (uxtheme+0x37)
00000000`0244f2b0  00000000`01bd0158
00000000`0244f2b8  00000000`00000082
00000000`0244f2c0  00000000`00000000
00000000`0244f2c8  00000000`00000003
00000000`0244f2d0  00000000`000111f2
00000000`0244f2d8  00000000`00000054
00000000`0244f2e0  00000000`00000000
00000000`0244f2e8  00000000`00000000
00000000`0244f2f0  00000000`00000001
00000000`0244f2f8  00000000`01c11c60
00000000`0244f300  00000000`0244f462
00000000`0244f308  00000000`01bd0230
00000000`0244f310  00000000`00000000
00000000`0244f318  00000000`00000000
00000000`0244f320  00000000`00000000
00000000`0244f328  00000000`14010015
00000000`0244f330  00000000`01c11570
00000000`0244f338  00000000`00000000
00000000`0244f340  00000000`00000000
00000000`0244f348  00000000`00000000
00000000`0244f350  00000000`00009c40
00000000`0244f358  00000000`00000000
00000000`0244f360  00000000`00000000
00000000`0244f368  00000000`00000000
00000000`0244f370  00000000`00002710
00000000`0244f378  00000000`77111248  ntdll!KiUserExceptionDispatch+0x2e
00000000`0244f380  00000000`0244f870
00000000`0244f388  00000000`0244f380
00000000`0244f390  00000000`00000000
00000000`0244f398  00000000`00000000
00000000`0244f3a0  000007fe`fb63fb40  uxtheme!$$VProc_ImageExportDirectory
00000000`0244f3a8  00000000`00000ad5
00000000`0244f3b0  00001f80`0010005f
00000000`0244f3b8  0053002b`002b0033
00000000`0244f3c0  00010246`002b002b
00000000`0244f3c8  00000000`00000000
00000000`0244f3d0  00000000`00000000
00000000`0244f3d8  00000000`00000000
00000000`0244f3e0  00000000`00000000
00000000`0244f3e8  00000000`00000000
00000000`0244f3f0  00000000`00000000
00000000`0244f3f8  00000000`0012c770
00000000`0244f400  00000000`00000000
00000000`0244f408  00000000`00000000
```

```
00000000`0244f410  00000000`00002710
00000000`0244f418  00000000`0244fab0
00000000`0244f420  00000000`00000000
00000000`0244f428  00000000`00000000
00000000`0244f430  00000000`00000000
00000000`0244f438  00000000`0244f938
00000000`0244f440  00000000`00962210
00000000`0244f448  00000000`00000000
00000000`0244f450  00000000`0244f9a0
00000000`0244f458  00000000`00009c40
00000000`0244f460  00000000`00000000
00000000`0244f468  00000000`00000000
00000000`0244f470  00000000`00000000
00000000`0244f478  00000000`ffdbdb27 calc!CTimedCalc::WatchDogThread+0xb2
00000000`0244f480  00000000`0000027f
00000000`0244f488  00000000`00000000
00000000`0244f490  00000000`00000000
00000000`0244f498  0000ffff`00001f80
00000000`0244f4a0  00000000`00000000
00000000`0244f4a8  00000000`00000000
00000000`0244f4b0  00000000`00000000
00000000`0244f4b8  00000000`00000000
00000000`0244f4c0  00000000`00000000
00000000`0244f4c8  00000000`00000000
00000000`0244f4d0  00000000`00000000
00000000`0244f4d8  00000000`00000000
00000000`0244f4e0  00000000`00000000
00000000`0244f4e8  00000000`00000000
00000000`0244f4f0  00000000`00000000
00000000`0244f4f8  00000000`00000000
00000000`0244f500  00000000`00000000
00000000`0244f508  00000000`00000000
00000000`0244f510  00000000`00000000
00000000`0244f518  00000000`00000000
00000000`0244f520  00000000`00000000
00000000`0244f528  00000000`00000000
00000000`0244f530  00000000`00000000
00000000`0244f538  00000000`00000000
00000000`0244f540  00000000`00000000
00000000`0244f548  00000000`00000000
00000000`0244f550  00000000`00000000
00000000`0244f558  00000000`00000000
00000000`0244f560  00000000`00000000
00000000`0244f568  00000000`00000000
00000000`0244f570  00000000`00000000
00000000`0244f578  00000000`00000000
00000000`0244f580  00000000`00000000
00000000`0244f588  00000000`00000000
00000000`0244f590  00000000`00000000
00000000`0244f598  00000000`00000000
00000000`0244f5a0  00000000`00000000
00000000`0244f5a8  00000000`00000000
00000000`0244f5b0  00000000`00000000
00000000`0244f5b8  00000000`00000000
00000000`0244f5c0  00000000`00000000
00000000`0244f5c8  00000000`00000000
00000000`0244f5d0  00000000`00000000
00000000`0244f5d8  00000000`00000000
00000000`0244f5e0  00000000`00000000
00000000`0244f5e8  00000000`00000000
```

```
00000000`0244f5f0  00000000`00000000
00000000`0244f5f8  00000000`00000000
00000000`0244f600  00000000`00000000
00000000`0244f608  00000000`00000000
00000000`0244f610  00000000`00000000
00000000`0244f618  00000000`00000000
00000000`0244f620  00000000`00000000
00000000`0244f628  00000000`00000000
00000000`0244f630  00000000`00000000
00000000`0244f638  00000000`00000000
00000000`0244f640  00000000`00000000
00000000`0244f648  00000000`00000000
00000000`0244f650  00000000`00000000
00000000`0244f658  00000000`00000000
00000000`0244f660  00000000`00000000
00000000`0244f668  fffff800`032d5e53
00000000`0244f670  00000000`00000002
00000000`0244f678  00000000`00000000
00000000`0244f680  00000000`01c11580
00000000`0244f688  00000000`00000082
00000000`0244f690  00000000`00000082
00000000`0244f698  00000000`000111e4
00000000`0244f6a0  00000000`00000002
00000000`0244f6a8  00000000`0244f6f0
00000000`0244f6b0  00000000`00000002
00000000`0244f6b8  00000000`00000000
00000000`0244f6c0  00000000`000111e4
00000000`0244f6c8  00000000`00000000
00000000`0244f6d0  00000000`00000082
00000000`0244f6d8  00000000`00000000
00000000`0244f6e0  00000000`00000000
00000000`0244f6e8  00000000`76fe76c2 user32!DefDlgProcW+0×36
00000000`0244f6f0  00000000`00000000
00000000`0244f6f8  00000000`00000000
00000000`0244f700  00000000`000111e4
00000000`0244f708  00000000`00000000
00000000`0244f710  00000000`00000082
00000000`0244f718  00000000`00000000
00000000`0244f720  00000000`0244f908
00000000`0244f728  00000000`76fd9bef user32!UserCallWinProcCheckWow+0×1cb
00000000`0244f730  00000000`00962210
00000000`0244f738  00000000`00000001
00000000`0244f740  00000000`00000000
00000000`0244f748  00000000`00000000
00000000`0244f750  00000000`0244f768
00000000`0244f758  00000000`0244f778
00000000`0244f760  00000000`00000001
00000000`0244f768  00000000`00000000
00000000`0244f770  00000000`00000000
00000000`0244f778  00000000`00000000
00000000`0244f780  00000000`00000048
00000000`0244f788  00000000`00000001
00000000`0244f790  00000000`00000000
00000000`0244f798  00000000`00000000
00000000`0244f7a0  00000000`00000070
00000000`0244f7a8  ffffffff`ffffffff
00000000`0244f7b0  ffffffff`ffffffff
00000000`0244f7b8  00000000`76fd9b43 user32!UserCallWinProcCheckWow+0×99
00000000`0244f7c0  00000000`76fd9bef user32!UserCallWinProcCheckWow+0×1cb
00000000`0244f7c8  00000000`00000000
```

```
00000000`0244f7d0  00000000`00000000
00000000`0244f7d8  00000000`00000000
00000000`0244f7e0  00000000`00000000
00000000`0244f7e8  00000000`76fd72cb user32!DispatchClientMessage+0xc3
00000000`0244f7f0  00000000`00000000
00000000`0244f7f8  00000000`770e46b4 ntdll!NtdllDialogWndProc_W
00000000`0244f800  00000000`00000000
00000000`0244f808  00000000`00000000
00000000`0244f810  00000000`00000000
00000000`0244f818  00000000`00000000
00000000`0244f820  00000000`00962238
00000000`0244f828  00000000`00000001
00000000`0244f830  00000000`00000000
00000000`0244f838  00000000`00000000
00000000`0244f840  00000000`00000000
00000000`0244f848  00000000`00000000
00000000`0244f850  00000730`fffffb30
00000000`0244f858  000004d0`fffffb30
00000000`0244f860  00000170`000000f0
00000000`0244f868  0000002c`00000001
00000000`0244f870  00000000`c0000005
00000000`0244f878  00000000`00000000
00000000`0244f880  00000000`ffdbdb27 calc!CTimedCalc::WatchDogThread+0xb2
00000000`0244f888  00000000`00000002
00000000`0244f890  00000000`00000000
00000000`0244f898  00000000`00000000
00000000`0244f8a0  00000000`00000000
00000000`0244f8a8  00000000`00000000
00000000`0244f8b0  00000000`00000000
00000000`0244f8b8  00000000`00000000
00000000`0244f8c0  00000000`00000000
00000000`0244f8c8  00000000`00000000
00000000`0244f8d0  00000000`00000000
00000000`0244f8d8  00000000`00000000
00000000`0244f8e0  00000000`00000000
00000000`0244f8e8  00000000`00000000
00000000`0244f8f0  00000000`00000000
00000000`0244f8f8  00000000`00000000
00000000`0244f900  00000000`00000000
00000000`0244f908  00000000`00962210
00000000`0244f910  00000000`ffdbdb27 calc!CTimedCalc::WatchDogThread+0xb2
00000000`0244f918  00000000`00000000
00000000`0244f920  00000000`00000000
00000000`0244f928  00000000`0244fab0
00000000`0244f930  00000000`77101530 ntdll!NtdllDispatchMessage_W
00000000`0244f938  00000000`76fe505b user32!DialogBox2+0x2ec
00000000`0244f940  00000000`00000000
00000000`0244f948  00000000`00000000
00000000`0244f950  00000000`00000000
00000000`0244f958  00000000`00000000
00000000`0244f960  00000000`00000000
00000000`0244f968  00000000`00000000
00000000`0244f970  00000000`00000000
00000000`0244f978  00000000`00000000
00000000`0244f980  00000000`00000002
00000000`0244f988  00000000`000111f0
00000000`0244f990  00000271`0f689359
00000000`0244f998  00000000`00000030
00000000`0244f9a0  00000000`00000000
00000000`0244f9a8  00000000`00000000
```

```
00000000`0244f9b0 00000000`ffd90000 calc!CCalculatorController::CCalculatorController <PERF>
(calc+0×0)
00000000`0244f9b8 00000000`001a17e0
00000000`0244f9c0 00000000`00000000
00000000`0244f9c8 00000000`76fe4edd user32!InternalDialogBox+0×135
00000000`0244f9d0 00000000`00000000
00000000`0244f9d8 00000000`ffdcedb0 calc!CTimedCalc::TimeOutDlgProc
00000000`0244f9e0 00000000`00000000
00000000`0244f9e8 00000000`00000000
00000000`0244f9f0 00000000`ffdcedb0 calc!CTimedCalc::TimeOutDlgProc
00000000`0244f9f8 00000000`00000000
00000000`0244fa00 00000000`00000001
00000000`0244fa08 00000000`00000000
00000000`0244fa10 00000000`00000000
00000000`0244fa18 00000000`00009c40
00000000`0244fa20 00000000`ffd90000 calc!CCalculatorController::CCalculatorController <PERF>
(calc+0×0)
00000000`0244fa28 00000000`76fe4f52 user32!DialogBoxIndirectParamAorW+0×58
00000000`0244fa30 00000000`001a17e0
00000000`0244fa38 00000000`00000000
00000000`0244fa40 00000000`ffdcedb0 calc!CTimedCalc::TimeOutDlgProc
00000000`0244fa48 00000000`ffdcedb0 calc!CTimedCalc::TimeOutDlgProc
00000000`0244fa50 00000000`00000000
00000000`0244fa58 00000000`00000001
00000000`0244fa60 00000000`ffd90000 calc!CCalculatorController::CCalculatorController <PERF>
(calc+0×0)
00000000`0244fa68 00000000`76fdd476 user32!DialogBoxParamW+0×66
00000000`0244fa70 ffffffff`ffffffff
00000000`0244fa78 00000000`00000000
00000000`0244fa80 00000000`ffdcedb0 calc!CTimedCalc::TimeOutDlgProc
00000000`0244fa88 00000000`00000000
00000000`0244fa90 00000000`00000000
00000000`0244fa98 00000000`00000000
00000000`0244faa0 00000000`00000000
00000000`0244faa8 00000000`ffdbdafa calc!CTimedCalc::WatchDogThread+0×72
00000000`0244fab0 00000000`00002710
```

Segment registers and flags now look normal:

```
0:003> .cxr 00000000`0244f380
rax=000000000012c770 rbx=0000000000002710 rcx=0000000000000000
rdx=0000000000000000 rsi=0000000000000000 rdi=0000000000000000
rip=00000000ffdbdb27 rsp=000000000244fab0 rbp=0000000000000000
r8=000000000244f938 r9=0000000000962210 r10=0000000000000000
r11=000000000244f9a0 r12=0000000000009c40 r13=0000000000000000
r14=0000000000000000 r15=0000000000000000
iopl=0 nv up ei pl zr na po nc
cs=0033 ss=002b ds=002b es=002b fs=0053 gs=002b efl=00010246
calc!CTimedCalc::WatchDogThread+0xb2:
00000000`ffdbdb27 488b01 mov rax,qword ptr [rcx] ds:00000000`00000000=????????????????


0:003> k
*** Stack trace for last set context - .thread/.cxr resets it
Child-SP RetAddr Call Site
00000000`0244fab0 00000000`76eb59ed calc!CTimedCalc::WatchDogThread+0xb2
00000000`0244faf0 00000000`770ec541 kernel32!BaseThreadInitThunk+0xd
00000000`0244fb20 00000000`00000000 ntdll!RtlUserThreadStart+0x1d
```

Patterns for Example B

- Heap Corruption
- Stack Trace Collection
- RIP Stack Trace
- Hooksware
- Patched Code
- Hidden Module
- Deviant Module
- String Hint
- Fake Module
- No Component Symbols
- Namespace

© 2014 Software Diagnostics Institute

This example is adapted with modifications from Accelerated Windows Malware Analysis training course for a different process memory dump.

We load a process memory dump:

```
Microsoft (R) Windows Debugger Version 6.3.9600.16384 AMD64
Copyright (c) Microsoft Corporation. All rights reserved.


Loading Dump File [C:\MemoryDumps\iexplore.exe.5152.dmp]
User Mini Dump File with Full Memory: Only application data is available


Symbol search path is: *** Invalid ***
************************************************************************
* Symbol loading may be unreliable without a symbol search path.       *
* Use .symfix to have the debugger choose a symbol path.               *
* After setting your symbol path, use .reload to refresh symbol locations. *
************************************************************************
Executable search path is:
Windows Server 2008/Windows Vista Version 6002 (Service Pack 2) MP (2 procs) Free x86
compatible
Product: WinNt, suite: SingleUserTS Personal
Machine Name:
Debug session time: Tue Sep 28 21:18:39.000 2010 (UTC + 1:00)
System Uptime: 1 days 8:45:34.374
Process Uptime: 0 days 0:19:42.000
...........................................................
...........................................................
.........
Loading unloaded module list
......
This dump file has an exception of interest stored in it.
The stored exception information can be accessed via .ecxr.
(1420.cf0): Unknown exception - code c0000374 (first/second chance not available)
*** ERROR: Symbol file could not be found.  Defaulted to export symbols for ntdll.dll -
eax=00000000 ebx=00000000 ecx=00000400 edx=00000000 esi=09a20000 edi=00001420
eip=77005e74 esp=06d2f37c ebp=06d2f400 iopl=0         nv up ei pl nz na pe nc
cs=001b  ss=0023  ds=0023  es=0023  fs=003b  gs=0000              efl=00000206
ntdll!KiFastSystemCallRet:
77005e74 c3                  ret
```

Note the message about **Stored Exception**.

We set up a link to Microsoft symbol server and reload symbols:

```
0:012> .symfix c:\mss

0:012> .reload
............................................................
............................................................
.........
Loading unloaded module list
......
```

We first check the current stack trace:

```
0:012> k
ChildEBP RetAddr
06d2f378 77005620 ntdll!KiFastSystemCallRet
06d2f37c 77033c62 ntdll!ZwWaitForSingleObject+0xc
06d2f400 77033d4b ntdll!RtlReportExceptionEx+0x14b
06d2f440 7704fa87 ntdll!RtlReportException+0x3c
06d2f454 7704fb0d ntdll!RtlpTerminateFailureFilter+0x14
06d2f460 76fa9bdc ntdll!RtlReportCriticalFailure+0x6b
06d2f474 76fa4067 ntdll!_EH4_CallFilterFunc+0x12
06d2f49c 77005f79 ntdll!_except_handler4+0x8e
06d2f4c0 77005f4b ntdll!ExecuteHandler2+0x26
06d2f570 77005dd7 ntdll!ExecuteHandler+0x24
06d2f570 7704faf8 ntdll!KiUserExceptionDispatcher+0xf
06d2f8e4 77050704 ntdll!RtlReportCriticalFailure+0x5b
06d2f8f4 770507f2 ntdll!RtlpReportHeapFailure+0x21
06d2f928 77050a64 ntdll!RtlpLogHeapFailure+0xa1
06d2f980 7701bafe ntdll!RtlpAnalyzeHeapFailure+0x25a
06d2fa6c 77006e0c ntdll!RtlpAllocateHeap+0x62f
06d2fae4 76fc4b2a ntdll!RtlAllocateHeap+0x1e3
06d2fbfc 76fddd4a ntdll!RtlpReAllocateHeap+0x864
06d2fc70 77115aac ntdll!RtlReAllocateHeap+0x2bf
06d2fcc4 73cb1d28 kernel32!GlobalReAlloc+0x2ba
06d2fcf0 73cb138b msacm32!mapWaveOpen+0x22f
06d2fd14 738e4d20 msacm32!wodMessage+0x79
06d2fd64 738e5215 winmm!waveOutOpen+0x280
06d2fdb4 738e4fe4 winmm!soundOpen+0xb1
06d2fdc4 738e5093 winmm!soundPlay+0x22
06d2fe00 738e14fc winmm!sndMessage+0x199
06d2fe34 7566fd72 winmm!mmWndProc+0x1a3
06d2fe60 7566fe4a user32!InternalCallWinProc+0x23
06d2fed8 7567018d user32!UserCallWinProcCheckWow+0x14b
06d2ff3c 75668b7c user32!DispatchMessageWorker+0x322
06d2ff4c 738e148c user32!DispatchMessageA+0xf
06d2ff78 7715d0e9 winmm!mciwindow+0xf9
06d2ff84 76fe19bb kernel32!BaseThreadInitThunk+0xe
06d2ffc4 76fe198e ntdll!__RtlUserThreadStart+0x23
06d2ffdc 00000000 ntdll!_RtlUserThreadStart+0x1b
```

We see **Heap Corruption** (or process **Dynamic Memory Corruption**) diagnostics. The usual impulse here is to enable full page heap and collect a new dump. But now analyze the memory dump a bit further.

Let's check **Stack Trace Collection** from all process threads:

```
0:012> ~*k

   0  Id: 1420.113c Suspend: 1 Teb: 7ffdf000 Unfrozen
ChildEBP RetAddr
001ef764 77005610 ntdll!KiFastSystemCallRet
001ef768 7715a5d7 ntdll!ZwWaitForMultipleObjects+0xc
001ef804 75670f8d kernel32!WaitForMultipleObjectsEx+0x11d
001ef858 7649334a user32!RealMsgWaitForMultipleObjectsEx+0x13c
001ef8a8 76494942 iertutil!IsoDispatchMessageToArtifacts+0x22c
001ef8c8 7016416a iertutil!IsoManagerThreadZero_WindowsPump+0x52
001ef918 008512e3 ieframe!LCIEStartAsTabProcess+0x25f
001efa64 0085147a iexplore!wWinMain+0x368
```

```
001efaf8 7715d0e9 iexplore!_initterm_e+0x1b1
001efb04 76fe19bb kernel32!BaseThreadInitThunk+0xe
001efb44 76fe198e ntdll!__RtlUserThreadStart+0x23
001efb5c 00000000 ntdll!_RtlUserThreadStart+0x1b

   1  Id: 1420.a54 Suspend: 1 Teb: 7ffde000 Unfrozen
ChildEBP RetAddr
01f6fb80 77005610 ntdll!KiFastSystemCallRet
01f6fb84 76fe2934 ntdll!ZwWaitForMultipleObjects+0xc
01f6fd18 7715d0e9 ntdll!TppWaiterpThread+0x328
01f6fd24 76fe19bb kernel32!BaseThreadInitThunk+0xe
01f6fd64 76fe198e ntdll!__RtlUserThreadStart+0x23
01f6fd7c 00000000 ntdll!_RtlUserThreadStart+0x1b

   2  Id: 1420.1544 Suspend: 1 Teb: 7ffdc000 Unfrozen
ChildEBP RetAddr
0234eb6c 77005610 ntdll!KiFastSystemCallRet
0234eb70 7715a5d7 ntdll!ZwWaitForMultipleObjects+0xc
0234ec0c 7715a6f0 kernel32!WaitForMultipleObjectsEx+0x11d
0234ec28 7648f08c kernel32!WaitForMultipleObjects+0x18
0234fc54 76494819 iertutil!CForeignProcessToCurrentProcessMessaging::_vThreadProc+0xa1
0234fc5c 7715d0e9 iertutil!CForeignProcessToCurrentProcessMessaging::_sThreadProc+0xd
0234fc68 76fe19bb kernel32!BaseThreadInitThunk+0xe
0234fca8 76fe198e ntdll!__RtlUserThreadStart+0x23
0234fcc0 00000000 ntdll!_RtlUserThreadStart+0x1b

   3  Id: 1420.bb8 Suspend: 1 Teb: 7ffdb000 Unfrozen
ChildEBP RetAddr
0250fdb4 77005610 ntdll!KiFastSystemCallRet
0250fdb8 7715a5d7 ntdll!ZwWaitForMultipleObjects+0xc
0250fe54 75670f8d kernel32!WaitForMultipleObjectsEx+0x11d
0250fea8 7649334a user32!RealMsgWaitForMultipleObjectsEx+0x13c
0250fef8 764948b6 iertutil!IsoDispatchMessageToArtifacts+0x22c
0250ff18 7715d0e9 iertutil!IsoManagerThreadNonzero_WindowsPump+0x59
0250ff24 76fe19bb kernel32!BaseThreadInitThunk+0xe
0250ff64 76fe198e ntdll!__RtlUserThreadStart+0x23
0250ff7c 00000000 ntdll!_RtlUserThreadStart+0x1b

   4  Id: 1420.16c8 Suspend: 1 Teb: 7ffda000 Unfrozen
ChildEBP RetAddr
028bd934 7567073f ntdll!KiFastSystemCallRet
028bd938 701ec23a user32!NtUserWaitMessage+0xc
028bfa3c 7019337e ieframe!CTabWindow::_TabWindowThreadProc+0x633
028bfaf4 7649426d ieframe!LCIETab_ThreadProc+0x2c1
028bfb04 7715d0e9 iertutil!CIsoScope::RegisterThread+0xab
028bfb10 76fe19bb kernel32!BaseThreadInitThunk+0xe
028bfb50 76fe198e ntdll!__RtlUserThreadStart+0x23
028bfb68 00000000 ntdll!_RtlUserThreadStart+0x1b

   5  Id: 1420.17d8 Suspend: 1 Teb: 7ffd9000 Unfrozen
ChildEBP RetAddr
029cf41c 77005610 ntdll!KiFastSystemCallRet
029cf420 7715a5d7 ntdll!ZwWaitForMultipleObjects+0xc
029cf4bc 7715a6f0 kernel32!WaitForMultipleObjectsEx+0x11d
*** ERROR: Symbol file could not be found.  Defaulted to export symbols for msidcrl40.dll -
029cf4d8 275c55c0 kernel32!WaitForMultipleObjects+0x18
WARNING: Stack unwind information not available. Following frames may be wrong.
029cf620 76fe4123 msidcrl40!CreatePassportAuthUIContext+0x2ab30
029cf65c 76fe3e23 ntdll!RtlpTpTimerCallback+0x62
029cf680 76fe2fcf ntdll!TppTimerpExecuteCallback+0x14d
```

```
029cf7b0 7715d0e9 ntdll!TppWorkerThread+0x545
029cf7bc 76fe19bb kernel32!BaseThreadInitThunk+0xe
029cf7fc 76fe198e ntdll!__RtlUserThreadStart+0x23
029cf814 00000000 ntdll!_RtlUserThreadStart+0x1b

   6  Id: 1420.60c Suspend: 1 Teb: 7ffd4000 Unfrozen
ChildEBP RetAddr
03d0f830 770057b0 ntdll!KiFastSystemCallRet
03d0f834 76fe2eb0 ntdll!NtWaitForWorkViaWorkerFactory+0xc
03d0f964 7715d0e9 ntdll!TppWorkerThread+0x1f6
03d0f970 76fe19bb kernel32!BaseThreadInitThunk+0xe
03d0f9b0 76fe198e ntdll!__RtlUserThreadStart+0x23
03d0f9c8 00000000 ntdll!_RtlUserThreadStart+0x1b

   7  Id: 1420.a74 Suspend: 1 Teb: 7ffaf000 Unfrozen
ChildEBP RetAddr
03fffbf0 77005620 ntdll!KiFastSystemCallRet
03fffbf4 77159884 ntdll!ZwWaitForSingleObject+0xc
03fffc64 771597f2 kernel32!WaitForSingleObjectEx+0xbe
03fffc78 6c8da731 kernel32!WaitForSingleObject+0x12
03fffc98 6c840778 mshtml!CDwnTaskExec::ThreadExec+0x23c
03fffca0 6c84083b mshtml!CExecFT::ThreadProc+0x39
03fffcac 7715d0e9 mshtml!CExecFT::StaticThreadProc+0xe
03fffcb8 76fe19bb kernel32!BaseThreadInitThunk+0xe
03fffcf8 76fe198e ntdll!__RtlUserThreadStart+0x23
03fffd10 00000000 ntdll!_RtlUserThreadStart+0x1b

   8  Id: 1420.151c Suspend: 1 Teb: 7ffad000 Unfrozen
ChildEBP RetAddr
05adf750 77005620 ntdll!KiFastSystemCallRet
05adf754 77159884 ntdll!ZwWaitForSingleObject+0xc
05adf7c4 771597f2 kernel32!WaitForSingleObjectEx+0xbe
05adf7d8 6c8da731 kernel32!WaitForSingleObject+0x12
05adf7f8 6c840778 mshtml!CDwnTaskExec::ThreadExec+0x23c
05adf800 6c84083b mshtml!CExecFT::ThreadProc+0x39
05adf80c 7715d0e9 mshtml!CExecFT::StaticThreadProc+0xe
05adf818 76fe19bb kernel32!BaseThreadInitThunk+0xe
05adf858 76fe198e ntdll!__RtlUserThreadStart+0x23
05adf870 00000000 ntdll!_RtlUserThreadStart+0x1b

   9  Id: 1420.f64 Suspend: 1 Teb: 7ffac000 Unfrozen
ChildEBP RetAddr
05fbf878 77005620 ntdll!KiFastSystemCallRet
05fbf87c 77159884 ntdll!ZwWaitForSingleObject+0xc
05fbf8ec 771597f2 kernel32!WaitForSingleObjectEx+0xbe
05fbf900 6c8da731 kernel32!WaitForSingleObject+0x12
05fbf920 6c840778 mshtml!CDwnTaskExec::ThreadExec+0x23c
05fbf928 6c84083b mshtml!CExecFT::ThreadProc+0x39
05fbf934 7715d0e9 mshtml!CExecFT::StaticThreadProc+0xe
05fbf940 76fe19bb kernel32!BaseThreadInitThunk+0xe
05fbf980 76fe198e ntdll!__RtlUserThreadStart+0x23
05fbf998 00000000 ntdll!_RtlUserThreadStart+0x1b

  10  Id: 1420.680 Suspend: 1 Teb: 7ffab000 Unfrozen
ChildEBP RetAddr
0640f958 77005610 ntdll!KiFastSystemCallRet
0640f95c 7715a5d7 ntdll!ZwWaitForMultipleObjects+0xc
0640f9f8 7715a6f0 kernel32!WaitForMultipleObjectsEx+0x11d
0640fa14 275b4879 kernel32!WaitForMultipleObjects+0x18
WARNING: Stack unwind information not available. Following frames may be wrong.
```

```
0640fd38 275b4a58 msidcrl40!CreatePassportAuthUIContext+0x19de9
0640fd60 275c9655 msidcrl40!CreatePassportAuthUIContext+0x19fc8
0640fd98 275c96fa msidcrl40!CreatePassportAuthUIContext+0x2ebc5
0640fdac 76fe19bb msidcrl40!CreatePassportAuthUIContext+0x2ec6a
0640fdec 76fe198e ntdll!__RtlUserThreadStart+0x23
0640fe04 00000000 ntdll!_RtlUserThreadStart+0x1b

  11  Id: 1420.12a4 Suspend: 1 Teb: 7ffaa000 Unfrozen
ChildEBP RetAddr
0615f6fc 77005610 ntdll!KiFastSystemCallRet
0615f700 7715a5d7 ntdll!ZwWaitForMultipleObjects+0xc
0615f79c 7715a6f0 kernel32!WaitForMultipleObjectsEx+0x11d
0615f7b8 275b4879 kernel32!WaitForMultipleObjects+0x18
WARNING: Stack unwind information not available. Following frames may be wrong.
0615fadc 275b4a58 msidcrl40!CreatePassportAuthUIContext+0x19de9
0615fb04 275c9655 msidcrl40!CreatePassportAuthUIContext+0x19fc8
0615fb3c 275c96fa msidcrl40!CreatePassportAuthUIContext+0x2ebc5
0615fb50 76fe19bb msidcrl40!CreatePassportAuthUIContext+0x2ec6a
0615fb90 76fe198e ntdll!__RtlUserThreadStart+0x23
0615fba8 00000000 ntdll!_RtlUserThreadStart+0x1b

# 12  Id: 1420.cf0 Suspend: 0 Teb: 7ffa9000 Unfrozen
ChildEBP RetAddr
06d2f378 77005620 ntdll!KiFastSystemCallRet
06d2f37c 77033c62 ntdll!ZwWaitForSingleObject+0xc
06d2f400 77033d4b ntdll!RtlReportExceptionEx+0x14b
06d2f440 7704fa87 ntdll!RtlReportException+0x3c
06d2f454 7704fb0d ntdll!RtlpTerminateFailureFilter+0x14
06d2f460 76fa9bdc ntdll!RtlReportCriticalFailure+0x6b
06d2f474 76fa4067 ntdll!_EH4_CallFilterFunc+0x12
06d2f49c 77005f79 ntdll!_except_handler4+0x8e
06d2f4c0 77005f4b ntdll!ExecuteHandler2+0x26
06d2f570 77005dd7 ntdll!ExecuteHandler+0x24
06d2f570 7704faf8 ntdll!KiUserExceptionDispatcher+0xf
06d2f8e4 77050704 ntdll!RtlReportCriticalFailure+0x5b
06d2f8f4 770507f2 ntdll!RtlpReportHeapFailure+0x21
06d2f928 77050a64 ntdll!RtlpLogHeapFailure+0xa1
06d2f980 7701bafe ntdll!RtlpAnalyzeHeapFailure+0x25a
06d2fa6c 77006e0c ntdll!RtlpAllocateHeap+0x62f
06d2fae4 76fc4b2a ntdll!RtlAllocateHeap+0x1e3
06d2fbfc 76fddd4a ntdll!RtlpReAllocateHeap+0x864
06d2fc70 77115aac ntdll!RtlReAllocateHeap+0x2bf
06d2fcc4 73cb1d28 kernel32!GlobalReAlloc+0x2ba
06d2fcf0 73cb138b msacm32!mapWaveOpen+0x22f
06d2fd14 738e4d20 msacm32!wodMessage+0x79
06d2fd64 738e5215 winmm!waveOutOpen+0x280
06d2fdb4 738e4fe4 winmm!soundOpen+0xb1
06d2fdc4 738e5093 winmm!soundPlay+0x22
06d2fe00 738e14fc winmm!sndMessage+0x199
06d2fe34 7566fd72 winmm!mmWndProc+0x1a3
06d2fe60 7566fe4a user32!InternalCallWinProc+0x23
06d2fed8 7567018d user32!UserCallWinProcCheckWow+0x14b
06d2ff3c 75668b7c user32!DispatchMessageWorker+0x322
06d2ff4c 738e148c user32!DispatchMessageA+0xf
06d2ff78 7715d0e9 winmm!mciwindow+0xf9
06d2ff84 76fe19bb kernel32!BaseThreadInitThunk+0xe
06d2ffc4 76fe198e ntdll!__RtlUserThreadStart+0x23
06d2ffdc 00000000 ntdll!_RtlUserThreadStart+0x1b
```

```
  13  Id: 1420.12f8 Suspend: 1 Teb: 7ffa8000 Unfrozen
ChildEBP RetAddr
06f2fa5c 77005610 ntdll!KiFastSystemCallRet
06f2fa60 7715a5d7 ntdll!ZwWaitForMultipleObjects+0xc
06f2fafc 73804f1d kernel32!WaitForMultipleObjectsEx+0x11d
06f2fb34 73807e96 wdmaud!CWorker::_ThreadProc+0x5e
06f2fb40 7715d0e9 wdmaud!CWorker::_StaticThreadProc+0x18
06f2fb4c 76fe19bb kernel32!BaseThreadInitThunk+0xe
06f2fb8c 76fe198e ntdll!__RtlUserThreadStart+0x23
06f2fba4 00000000 ntdll!_RtlUserThreadStart+0x1b

  14  Id: 1420.162c Suspend: 1 Teb: 7ffa7000 Unfrozen
ChildEBP RetAddr
06e2f95c 77005620 ntdll!KiFastSystemCallRet
06e2f960 74c716c7 ntdll!ZwWaitForSingleObject+0xc
06e2f9a0 74c7179d mswsock!SockWaitForSingleObject+0x3a
06e2fa8c 76521693 mswsock!WSPSelect+0x38c
06e2fb0c 7670e9a9 ws2_32!select+0x494
06e2fe64 7672deab wininet!ICAsyncThread::SelectThread+0x242
06e2fe6c 7715d0e9 wininet!ICAsyncThread::SelectThreadWrapper+0xd
06e2fe78 76fe19bb kernel32!BaseThreadInitThunk+0xe
06e2feb8 76fe198e ntdll!__RtlUserThreadStart+0x23
06e2fed0 00000000 ntdll!_RtlUserThreadStart+0x1b

  15  Id: 1420.bd0 Suspend: 1 Teb: 7ffa6000 Unfrozen
ChildEBP RetAddr
0748fb18 770050b0 ntdll!KiFastSystemCallRet
0748fb1c 74c764f1 ntdll!NtRemoveIoCompletion+0xc
0748fb54 7715d0e9 mswsock!SockAsyncThread+0x69
0748fb60 76fe19bb kernel32!BaseThreadInitThunk+0xe
0748fba0 76fe198e ntdll!__RtlUserThreadStart+0x23
0748fbb8 00000000 ntdll!_RtlUserThreadStart+0x1b

  16  Id: 1420.10a4 Suspend: 1 Teb: 7ffd6000 Unfrozen
ChildEBP RetAddr
02b2fdd8 77004780 ntdll!KiFastSystemCallRet
02b2fddc 77159990 ntdll!NtDelayExecution+0xc
02b2fe44 77111c6c kernel32!SleepEx+0x62
02b2fe54 76e93f1d kernel32!Sleep+0xf
02b2fe60 76eaeb46 ole32!CROIDTable::WorkerThreadLoop+0x14
[d:\longhorn\com\ole32\com\dcomrem\refcache.cxx @ 1345]
02b2fe7c 76e957ab ole32!CRpcThread::WorkerLoop+0x26
[d:\longhorn\com\ole32\com\dcomrem\threads.cxx @ 257]
02b2fe8c 7715d0e9 ole32!CRpcThreadCache::RpcWorkerThreadEntry+0x16
[d:\longhorn\com\ole32\com\dcomrem\threads.cxx @ 63]
02b2fe98 76fe19bb kernel32!BaseThreadInitThunk+0xe
02b2fed8 76fe198e ntdll!__RtlUserThreadStart+0x23
02b2fef0 00000000 ntdll!_RtlUserThreadStart+0x1b

  17  Id: 1420.8f0 Suspend: 1 Teb: 7ff9f000 Unfrozen
ChildEBP RetAddr
093efb78 7567073f ntdll!KiFastSystemCallRet
093efb7c 70278291 user32!NtUserWaitMessage+0xc
093efbb8 7025f3e0 ieframe!IEDownload_ThreadProc+0x17a
093efc28 7715d0e9 ieframe!WrapperThreadProc+0x9b
093efc34 76fe19bb kernel32!BaseThreadInitThunk+0xe
093efc74 76fe198e ntdll!__RtlUserThreadStart+0x23
093efc8c 00000000 ntdll!_RtlUserThreadStart+0x1b
```

```
  18  Id: 1420.1640 Suspend: 1 Teb: 7ffa5000 Unfrozen
ChildEBP RetAddr
0b52f934 7567073f ntdll!KiFastSystemCallRet
0b52f938 70278291 user32!NtUserWaitMessage+0xc
0b52f974 7025f3e0 ieframe!IEDownload_ThreadProc+0x17a
0b52f9e4 7715d0e9 ieframe!WrapperThreadProc+0x9b
0b52f9f0 76fe19bb kernel32!BaseThreadInitThunk+0xe
0b52fa30 76fe198e ntdll!__RtlUserThreadStart+0x23
0b52fa48 00000000 ntdll!_RtlUserThreadStart+0x1b

  19  Id: 1420.1270 Suspend: 1 Teb: 7ffd8000 Unfrozen
ChildEBP RetAddr
0765fb8c 770057b0 ntdll!KiFastSystemCallRet
0765fb90 76fe2eb0 ntdll!NtWaitForWorkViaWorkerFactory+0xc
0765fcc0 7715d0e9 ntdll!TppWorkerThread+0x1f6
0765fccc 76fe19bb kernel32!BaseThreadInitThunk+0xe
0765fd0c 76fe198e ntdll!__RtlUserThreadStart+0x23
0765fd24 00000000 ntdll!_RtlUserThreadStart+0x1b

  20  Id: 1420.11b0 Suspend: 1 Teb: 7ffd7000 Unfrozen
ChildEBP RetAddr
091ffe58 770050b0 ntdll!KiFastSystemCallRet
091ffe5c 7715d11e ntdll!NtRemoveIoCompletion+0xc
091ffe88 76bb03c8 kernel32!GetQueuedCompletionStatus+0x29
091ffec4 76bb04fd rpcrt4!COMMON_ProcessCalls+0xb5
091fff34 76bb011c rpcrt4!LOADABLE_TRANSPORT::ProcessIOEvents+0x138
091fff3c 76bb00e3 rpcrt4!ProcessIOEventsWrapper+0xd
091fff60 76bb0166 rpcrt4!BaseCachedThreadRoutine+0x5c
091fff6c 7715d0e9 rpcrt4!ThreadStartRoutine+0x1e
091fff78 76fe19bb kernel32!BaseThreadInitThunk+0xe
091fffb8 76fe198e ntdll!__RtlUserThreadStart+0x23
091fffd0 00000000 ntdll!_RtlUserThreadStart+0x1b

  21  Id: 1420.163c Suspend: 1 Teb: 7ffdd000 Unfrozen
ChildEBP RetAddr
095efcb8 770057b0 ntdll!KiFastSystemCallRet
095efcbc 76fe2eb0 ntdll!NtWaitForWorkViaWorkerFactory+0xc
095efdec 7715d0e9 ntdll!TppWorkerThread+0x1f6
095efdf8 76fe19bb kernel32!BaseThreadInitThunk+0xe
095efe38 76fe198e ntdll!__RtlUserThreadStart+0x23
095efe50 00000000 ntdll!_RtlUserThreadStart+0x1b

  22  Id: 1420.12ec Suspend: 1 Teb: 7ffd3000 Unfrozen
ChildEBP RetAddr
08f789a8 77005620 ntdll!KiFastSystemCallRet
08f789ac 76fde16a ntdll!ZwWaitForSingleObject+0xc
08f78a10 76fde04d ntdll!RtlpWaitOnCriticalSection+0x155
08f78a38 76fde6d8 ntdll!RtlEnterCriticalSection+0x152
08f78a6c 7712c119 ntdll!RtlLockHeap+0x3d
08f78aac 76af27bc kernel32!LocalReAlloc+0x51
08f78acc 76af28a2 advapi32!UnicodeToMultiByte+0x56
08f78c00 0005180f advapi32!GetCurrentHwProfileA+0x5d
WARNING: Frame IP not in any known module. Following frames may be wrong.
08f78c10 00050e8b 0x5180f
08f78dec 771d006c 0x50e8b
08f78ee8 00049e68 kernel32!WerpGetFlags+0x24
08f78fa4 76d3b7b1 0x49e68
08f78fe4 76d3b32b urlmon!CINetHttp::INetAsyncSendRequest+0x347
08f79804 76d3b4c8 urlmon!CINetHttp::INetAsyncOpenRequest+0x2cf
08f79818 76d3ac97 urlmon!CINet::INetAsyncConnect+0x24b
```

```
08f79830 76d26af9 urlmon!CINet::INetAsyncOpen+0x11b
08f79840 76d26aaa urlmon!CINet::INetAsyncStart+0x1a
08f7985c 76d2693f urlmon!CINet::StartCommon+0x198
08f79878 76d26b5e urlmon!CINet::StartEx+0x1c
08f798ac 76d18e84 urlmon!COInetProt::StartEx+0xc2
08f798fc 76d19411 urlmon!CTransaction::StartEx+0x3e1
08f79984 76d19022 urlmon!CBinding::StartBinding+0x602
08f799c8 76d19fc0 urlmon!CUrlMon::StartBinding+0x169
08f799f0 6c8deac6 urlmon!CUrlMon::BindToStorage+0x90
08f79a1c 6c8de9cb mshtml!CStreamProxy::Bind+0xce
08f79cbc 6c8db277 mshtml!CDwnBindData::Bind+0x74b
08f79ce4 6c8db118 mshtml!NewDwnBindData+0x15f
08f79d34 6c85f0aa mshtml!CDwnLoad::Init+0x121
08f79d88 6c8daa61 mshtml!CHtmLoad::Init+0x1fe
08f79dac 6c8da967 mshtml!CDwnInfo::SetLoad+0x119
08f79dcc 6c85e021 mshtml!CDwnCtx::SetLoad+0x7a
08f79de4 6c85ec7b mshtml!CHtmCtx::SetLoad+0x13
08f79e04 6c8525c9 mshtml!CMarkup::Load+0x167
08f7a008 6c9ff395 mshtml!CMarkup::LoadFromInfo+0xb5a
08f7a1e0 6c9ff532 mshtml!CDoc::DoNavigate+0x1508
08f7a300 6cc7557e mshtml!CDoc::FollowHyperlink2+0xda7
08f7a3c8 6cc75170 mshtml!CFormElement::DoSubmit+0x405
08f7a3dc 6c891bc5 mshtml!CFormElement::submit+0x11
08f7a3f8 6c91adc3 mshtml!Method_void_void+0x75
08f7a46c 6c926e11 mshtml!CBase::ContextInvokeEx+0x5d1
08f7a4bc 6ca19057 mshtml!CElement::ContextInvokeEx+0x9d
08f7a4f8 6c91a7c1 mshtml!CFormElement::VersionedInvokeEx+0xf0
08f7a548 6c25392a mshtml!PlainInvokeEx+0xea
08f7a588 6c253876 jscript!IDispatchExInvokeEx2+0xf8
08f7a5c4 6c254db6 jscript!IDispatchExInvokeEx+0x6a
08f7a684 6c254d10 jscript!InvokeDispatchEx+0x98
08f7a6b8 6c252bfd jscript!VAR::InvokeByName+0x135
08f7a704 6c2540c5 jscript!VAR::InvokeDispName+0x7a
08f7a734 6c254e23 jscript!VAR::InvokeByDispID+0xce
08f7a8d0 6c25123b jscript!CScriptRuntime::Run+0x2abe
08f7a9b8 6c251175 jscript!ScrFncObj::CallWithFrameOnStack+0xff
08f7aa04 6c25493c jscript!ScrFncObj::Call+0x8f
08f7aa88 6c252755 jscript!NameTbl::InvokeInternal+0x137
08f7aabc 6c252fa4 jscript!VAR::InvokeByDispID+0x17c
08f7ac58 6c25123b jscript!CScriptRuntime::Run+0x29e0
08f7ad40 6c251175 jscript!ScrFncObj::CallWithFrameOnStack+0xff
08f7ad8c 6c250fa3 jscript!ScrFncObj::Call+0x8f
08f7ae08 6c233ea3 jscript!CSession::Execute+0x175
08f7ae54 6c23552f jscript!COleScript::ExecutePendingScripts+0x1c0
08f7aeb8 6c235345 jscript!COleScript::ParseScriptTextCore+0x29a
08f7aee0 6c85a304 jscript!COleScript::ParseScriptText+0x30
08f7af38 6ca254c2 mshtml!CScriptCollection::ParseScriptText+0x219
08f7cfd0 6ca0a568 mshtml!CWindow::ExecuteScriptUri+0x19f
08f7d018 6ca25810 mshtml!CWindow::NavigateEx+0x5a
08f7d084 6ca256b5 mshtml!CDoc::ExecuteScriptUri+0x262
08f7d0c0 6caf6b68 mshtml!CDoc::ExecuteScriptURL+0x4e
08f7d114 6c9641a7 mshtml!CHyperlink::ClickAction+0x269
08f7d124 6cc3c96f mshtml!CAnchorElement::ClickAction+0x10
08f7d14c 6c96416e mshtml!CImgElement::ClickAction+0x6c
08f7d180 6c9601ff mshtml!CElement::DoClick+0x155
08f7d21c 6ca3e941 mshtml!CDoc::PumpMessage+0xf63
08f7d394 6c964408 mshtml!CDoc::OnMouseMessage+0x55d
08f7d4c0 6c939241 mshtml!CDoc::OnWindowMessage+0x9d9
08f7d4ec 7566fd72 mshtml!CServer::WndProc+0x78
08f7d518 7566fe4a user32!InternalCallWinProc+0x23
```

```
08f7d590 756709d3 user32!UserCallWinProcCheckWow+0x14b
08f7d5c0 75670979 user32!CallWindowProcAorW+0x97
*** ERROR: Symbol file could not be found.  Defaulted to export symbols for
rpbrowserrecordplugin.dll -
08f7d5e0 633da439 user32!CallWindowProcW+0x1b
08f7d600 633d6ee9 rpbrowserrecordplugin+0xa439
08f7d628 7566fd72 rpbrowserrecordplugin+0x6ee9
08f7d654 7566fe4a user32!InternalCallWinProc+0x23
08f7d6cc 7567018d user32!UserCallWinProcCheckWow+0x14b
08f7d730 7567022b user32!DispatchMessageWorker+0x322
08f7d740 701ec1d5 user32!DispatchMessageW+0xf
08f7f848 7019337e ieframe!CTabWindow::_TabWindowThreadProc+0x54c
08f7f900 7649426d ieframe!LCIETab_ThreadProc+0x2c1
08f7f910 7715d0e9 iertutil!CIsoScope::RegisterThread+0xab
08f7f91c 76fe19bb kernel32!BaseThreadInitThunk+0xe
08f7f95c 76fe198e ntdll!__RtlUserThreadStart+0x23
08f7f974 00000000 ntdll!_RtlUserThreadStart+0x1b

  23  Id: 1420.1670 Suspend: 1 Teb: 7ffae000 Unfrozen
ChildEBP RetAddr
0997f940 770050b0 ntdll!KiFastSystemCallRet
0997f944 7715d11e ntdll!NtRemoveIoCompletion+0xc
0997f970 76bb03c8 kernel32!GetQueuedCompletionStatus+0x29
0997f9ac 76bb04fd rpcrt4!COMMON_ProcessCalls+0xb5
0997fa1c 76bb011c rpcrt4!LOADABLE_TRANSPORT::ProcessIOEvents+0x138
0997fa24 76bb00e3 rpcrt4!ProcessIOEventsWrapper+0xd
0997fa48 76bb0166 rpcrt4!BaseCachedThreadRoutine+0x5c
0997fa54 7715d0e9 rpcrt4!ThreadStartRoutine+0x1e
0997fa60 76fe19bb kernel32!BaseThreadInitThunk+0xe
0997faa0 76fe198e ntdll!__RtlUserThreadStart+0x23
0997fab8 00000000 ntdll!_RtlUserThreadStart+0x1b

  24  Id: 1420.15e0 Suspend: 1 Teb: 7ffa4000 Unfrozen
ChildEBP RetAddr
09b5f7b8 770050b0 ntdll!KiFastSystemCallRet
09b5f7bc 7715d11e ntdll!NtRemoveIoCompletion+0xc
09b5f7e8 76bb03c8 kernel32!GetQueuedCompletionStatus+0x29
09b5f824 76bb04fd rpcrt4!COMMON_ProcessCalls+0xb5
09b5f894 76bb011c rpcrt4!LOADABLE_TRANSPORT::ProcessIOEvents+0x138
09b5f89c 76bb00e3 rpcrt4!ProcessIOEventsWrapper+0xd
09b5f8c0 76bb0166 rpcrt4!BaseCachedThreadRoutine+0x5c
09b5f8cc 7715d0e9 rpcrt4!ThreadStartRoutine+0x1e
09b5f8d8 76fe19bb kernel32!BaseThreadInitThunk+0xe
09b5f918 76fe198e ntdll!__RtlUserThreadStart+0x23
09b5f930 00000000 ntdll!_RtlUserThreadStart+0x1b

  25  Id: 1420.16f4 Suspend: 1 Teb: 7ffa3000 Unfrozen
ChildEBP RetAddr
090ef72c 770057b0 ntdll!KiFastSystemCallRet
090ef730 76fe2eb0 ntdll!NtWaitForWorkViaWorkerFactory+0xc
090ef860 7715d0e9 ntdll!TppWorkerThread+0x1f6
090ef86c 76fe19bb kernel32!BaseThreadInitThunk+0xe
090ef8ac 76fe198e ntdll!__RtlUserThreadStart+0x23
090ef8c4 00000000 ntdll!_RtlUserThreadStart+0x1b
```

```
   26  Id: 1420.13e8 Suspend: 1 Teb: 7ffa2000 Unfrozen
ChildEBP RetAddr
09ccf814 770057b0 ntdll!KiFastSystemCallRet
09ccf818 76fe2eb0 ntdll!NtWaitForWorkViaWorkerFactory+0xc
09ccf948 7715d0e9 ntdll!TppWorkerThread+0x1f6
09ccf954 76fe19bb kernel32!BaseThreadInitThunk+0xe
09ccf994 76fe198e ntdll!__RtlUserThreadStart+0x23
09ccf9ac 00000000 ntdll!_RtlUserThreadStart+0x1b

   27  Id: 1420.d9c Suspend: 1 Teb: 7ffa1000 Unfrozen
ChildEBP RetAddr
0cd3fe60 77005620 ntdll!KiFastSystemCallRet
0cd3fe64 77159884 ntdll!ZwWaitForSingleObject+0xc
0cd3fed4 771597f2 kernel32!WaitForSingleObjectEx+0xbe
*** ERROR: Symbol file could not be found.  Defaulted to export symbols for Flash10k.ocx -
0cd3fee8 674cd4d8 kernel32!WaitForSingleObject+0x12
WARNING: Stack unwind information not available. Following frames may be wrong.
0cd3ff70 674cd5ec Flash10k!DllUnregisterServer+0x3db6a
0cd3ff90 76fe19bb Flash10k!DllUnregisterServer+0x3dc7e
0cd3ffd0 76fe198e ntdll!__RtlUserThreadStart+0x23
0cd3ffe8 00000000 ntdll!_RtlUserThreadStart+0x1b

   28  Id: 1420.12d4 Suspend: 1 Teb: 7ffa0000 Unfrozen
ChildEBP RetAddr
0ca4fb5c 77005620 ntdll!KiFastSystemCallRet
0ca4fb60 77159884 ntdll!ZwWaitForSingleObject+0xc
0ca4fbd0 771597f2 kernel32!WaitForSingleObjectEx+0xbe
0ca4fbe4 674cd4d8 kernel32!WaitForSingleObject+0x12
WARNING: Stack unwind information not available. Following frames may be wrong.
0ca4fc6c 674cd5ec Flash10k!DllUnregisterServer+0x3db6a
0ca4fc8c 76fe19bb Flash10k!DllUnregisterServer+0x3dc7e
0ca4fccc 76fe198e ntdll!__RtlUserThreadStart+0x23
0ca4fce4 00000000 ntdll!_RtlUserThreadStart+0x1b

   29  Id: 1420.10d8 Suspend: 1 Teb: 7ff9e000 Unfrozen
ChildEBP RetAddr
0d16f738 77005620 ntdll!KiFastSystemCallRet
0d16f73c 77159884 ntdll!ZwWaitForSingleObject+0xc
0d16f7ac 771597f2 kernel32!WaitForSingleObjectEx+0xbe
0d16f7c0 674cd4d8 kernel32!WaitForSingleObject+0x12
WARNING: Stack unwind information not available. Following frames may be wrong.
0d16f848 674cd5ec Flash10k!DllUnregisterServer+0x3db6a
0d16f868 76fe19bb Flash10k!DllUnregisterServer+0x3dc7e
0d16f8a8 76fe198e ntdll!__RtlUserThreadStart+0x23
0d16f8c0 00000000 ntdll!_RtlUserThreadStart+0x1b

   30  Id: 1420.1560 Suspend: 1 Teb: 7ff9d000 Unfrozen
ChildEBP RetAddr
0d4ff6c4 770057b0 ntdll!KiFastSystemCallRet
0d4ff6c8 76fe2eb0 ntdll!NtWaitForWorkViaWorkerFactory+0xc
0d4ff7f8 7715d0e9 ntdll!TppWorkerThread+0x1f6
0d4ff804 76fe19bb kernel32!BaseThreadInitThunk+0xe
0d4ff844 76fe198e ntdll!__RtlUserThreadStart+0x23
0d4ff85c 00000000 ntdll!_RtlUserThreadStart+0x1b
```

```
   31  Id: 1420.fd0 Suspend: 1 Teb: 7ff9c000 Unfrozen
ChildEBP RetAddr
0d65fae4 77005620 ntdll!KiFastSystemCallRet
0d65fae8 77159884 ntdll!ZwWaitForSingleObject+0xc
0d65fb58 771597f2 kernel32!WaitForSingleObjectEx+0xbe
0d65fb6c 6ca78fed kernel32!WaitForSingleObject+0x12
0d65fb90 6c840778 mshtml!CTimerMan::ThreadExec+0x90
0d65fb98 6c84083b mshtml!CExecFT::ThreadProc+0x39
0d65fba4 7715d0e9 mshtml!CExecFT::StaticThreadProc+0xe
0d65fbb0 76fe19bb kernel32!BaseThreadInitThunk+0xe
0d65fbf0 76fe198e ntdll!__RtlUserThreadStart+0x23
0d65fc08 00000000 ntdll!_RtlUserThreadStart+0x1b

   32  Id: 1420.1048 Suspend: 1 Teb: 7ff9b000 Unfrozen
ChildEBP RetAddr
0db5fda0 77005610 ntdll!KiFastSystemCallRet
0db5fda4 7715a5d7 ntdll!ZwWaitForMultipleObjects+0xc
0db5fe40 75670f8d kernel32!WaitForMultipleObjectsEx+0x11d
0db5fe94 75667f5a user32!RealMsgWaitForMultipleObjectsEx+0x13c
0db5feb0 73d674b2 user32!MsgWaitForMultipleObjects+0x1f
0db5fefc 7715d0e9 GdiPlus!BackgroundThreadProc+0x59
0db5ff08 76fe19bb kernel32!BaseThreadInitThunk+0xe
0db5ff48 76fe198e ntdll!__RtlUserThreadStart+0x23
0db5ff60 00000000 ntdll!_RtlUserThreadStart+0x1b
```

We see another thread #22 trying to enter a critical section when acessing process heap. What we also see are raw instruction pointers on the stack trace (**RIP Stack Trace**). This can often be seen in managed .NET execution environment with its JIT compiled .NET code. However there is no presence of .NET CLR modules such as mscorwks.dll or clr.dll on the stack trace.

Let's look at this RIP address closely by doing backwards disassembly:

```
0:012> ub 0x49e68
00049e50 52              push    edx
00049e51 e87a5a0000      call    0004f8d0
00049e56 6a01            push    1
00049e58 6a01            push    1
00049e5a 6898aa0500      push    5AA98h
00049e5f 8b45b8          mov     eax,dword ptr [ebp-48h]
00049e62 50              push    eax
00049e63 e848280000      call    0004c6b0

0:012> u 0004c6b0
0004c6b0 55              push    ebp
0004c6b1 8bec            mov     ebp,esp
0004c6b3 81ec78010000    sub     esp,178h
0004c6b9 56              push    esi
0004c6ba 57              push    edi
0004c6bb e8e07fffff      call    000446a0
0004c6c0 8945d8          mov     dword ptr [ebp-28h],eax
0004c6c3 837dd800        cmp     dword ptr [ebp-28h],0
```

Let's check the address attribute:

```
0:012> !address 0x49e68
```

```
Mapping file section regions...
Mapping module regions...
Mapping PEB regions...
Mapping TEB and stack regions...
Mapping heap regions...
Mapping page heap regions...
Mapping other regions...
Mapping stack trace database regions...
Mapping activation context regions...
```

```
Usage:                  <unknown>
Base Address:           00040000
End Address:            0005d000
Region Size:            0001d000
State:                  00001000 MEM_COMMIT
Protect:                00000040 PAGE_EXECUTE_READWRITE
Type:                   00020000 MEM_PRIVATE
Allocation Base:        00040000
Allocation Protect:     00000040 PAGE_EXECUTE_READWRITE
```

We see that the region is also writable compared to normal code:

```
0:012> !address 73d674b2
```

```
Usage:                  Image
Base Address:           73d51000
End Address:            73ed7000
Region Size:            00186000
State:                  00001000 MEM_COMMIT
Protect:                00000020 PAGE_EXECUTE_READ
Type:                   01000000 MEM_IMAGE
Allocation Base:        73d50000
Allocation Protect:     00000080 PAGE_EXECUTE_WRITECOPY
Image Path:
C:\Windows\winsxs\x86_microsoft.windows.gdiplus_6595b64144ccf1df_1.0.6002.18005_none_9e50b396ca
17ae07\GdiPlus.dll
Module Name:            GdiPlus
Loaded Image Name:      GdiPlus.dll
Mapped Image Name:
More info:              lmv m GdiPlus
More info:              !lmi GdiPlus
More info:              ln 0x73d674b2
More info:              !dh 0x73d50000
```

Now we check if the base address contains any module information:

```
0:012> dc 00040000
00040000   00905a4d 00000003 00000004 0000ffff   MZ..............
00040010   000000b8 00000000 00000040 00000000   ........@.......
00040020   00000000 00000000 00000000 00000000   ................
00040030   00000000 00000000 00000000 000000d8   ................
00040040   0eba1f0e cd09b400 4c01b821 685421cd   ........!..L.!Th
00040050   70207369 72676f72 63206d61 6f6e6e61   is program canno
00040060   65622074 6e757220 206e6920 20534f44   t be run in DOS
00040070   65646f6d 0a0d0d2e 00000024 00000000   mode....$.......

0:012> !dh 00040000

File Type: EXECUTABLE IMAGE
FILE HEADER VALUES
      14C machine (i386)
        4 number of sections
4C9E36D3 time date stamp Sat Sep 25 18:52:19 2010

        0 file pointer to symbol table
        0 number of symbols
       E0 size of optional header
      102 characteristics
             Executable
             32 bit word machine

OPTIONAL HEADER VALUES
      10B magic #
     9.00 linker version
    12200 size of code
     7000 size of initialized data
        0 size of uninitialized data
     D5F0 address of entry point
     1000 base of code
          ----- new -----
 00400000 image base
     1000 section alignment
      200 file alignment
        2 subsystem (Windows GUI)
     5.00 operating system version
     0.00 image version
     5.00 subsystem version
    1D000 size of image
      400 size of headers
        0 checksum
 00100000 size of stack reserve
 00001000 size of stack commit
 00100000 size of heap reserve
 00001000 size of heap commit
     8540 DLL characteristics
             Dynamic base
             NX compatible
             No structured exception handler
             Terminal server aware
        0 [        0] address [size] of Export Directory
        0 [        0] address [size] of Import Directory
        0 [        0] address [size] of Resource Directory
        0 [        0] address [size] of Exception Directory
```

55

```
       0 [        0] address [size] of Security Directory
   1C000 [      3F0] address [size] of Base Relocation Directory
       0 [        0] address [size] of Debug Directory
       0 [        0] address [size] of Description Directory
       0 [        0] address [size] of Special Directory
       0 [        0] address [size] of Thread Storage Directory
       0 [        0] address [size] of Load Configuration Directory
       0 [        0] address [size] of Bound Import Directory
       0 [        0] address [size] of Import Address Table Directory
       0 [        0] address [size] of Delay Import Directory
       0 [        0] address [size] of COR20 Header Directory
       0 [        0] address [size] of Reserved Directory


SECTION HEADER #1
   .text name
   1203B virtual size
    1000 virtual address
   12200 size of raw data
     400 file pointer to raw data
       0 file pointer to relocation table
       0 file pointer to line numbers
       0 number of relocations
       0 number of line numbers
60000020 flags
         Code
         (no align specified)
         Execute Read


SECTION HEADER #2
   .rdata name
     7D0 virtual size
   14000 virtual address
     800 size of raw data
   12600 file pointer to raw data
       0 file pointer to relocation table
       0 file pointer to line numbers
       0 number of relocations
       0 number of line numbers
40000040 flags
         Initialized Data
         (no align specified)
         Read Only


SECTION HEADER #3
   .data name
    6008 virtual size
   15000 virtual address
    4000 size of raw data
   12E00 file pointer to raw data
       0 file pointer to relocation table
       0 file pointer to line numbers
       0 number of relocations
       0 number of line numbers
C0000040 flags
         Initialized Data
         (no align specified)
         Read Write
```

```
SECTION HEADER #4
  .reloc name
     5F0 virtual size
   1C000 virtual address
     600 size of raw data
   16E00 file pointer to raw data
       0 file pointer to relocation table
       0 file pointer to line numbers
       0 number of relocations
       0 number of line numbers
42000040 flags
         Initialized Data
         Discardable
         (no align specified)
         Read Only
```

We see this **Deviant Module** doesn't have any import tables.

We now check the module range for any **String Hints**:

```
0:012> s-sa 00040000 0005d000
0004004d  "!This program cannot be run in D"
0004006d  "OS mode."
00040081  "3y@"
000400b8  "Rich"
000401d0  ".text"
000401f7  "`.rdata"
0004021f  "@.data"
00040248  ".reloc"
[...]
00054000  "HELLO"
00054008  "%s:%s"
00054010  "READY"
00054018  "GET /stat?uptime=%d&downlink=%d&"
00054038  "uplink=%d&id=%s&statpass=%s&comm"
00054058  "ent=%s HTTP/1.0"
000540ac  "%s%s%s"
000540d8  "ftp://%s:%s@%s:%d"
000540fc  "Accept-Encoding:"
00054118  "Accept-Encoding:"
00054130  "0123456789ABCDEF"
00054144  "://"
00054160  "POST %s HTTP/1.0"
00054172  "Host: %s"
0005417c  "User-Agent: %s"
0005418c  "Accept: text/html"
0005419f  "Connection: Close"
000541b2  "Content-Type: application/x-www-"
000541d2  "form-urlencoded"
000541e3  "Content-Length: %d"
000541fc  "id="
00054208  "POST %s HTTP/1.1"
0005421a  "Host: %s"
00054224  "User-Agent: %s"
00054234  "Accept: text/html"
00054247  "Connection: Close"
0005425a  "Content-Type: application/x-www-"
0005427a  "form-urlencoded"
0005428b  "Content-Length: %d"
```

```
000542a4   "id=%s&base="
000542b8   "id=%s&brw=%d&type=%d&data="
000542d8   "POST %s HTTP/1.1"
000542ea   "Host: %s"
000542f4   "User-Agent: %s"
00054304   "Accept: text/html"
00054317   "Connection: Close"
0005432a   "Content-Type: application/x-www-"
0005434a   "form-urlencoded"
0005435b   "Content-Length: %d"
00054378   "id=%s&os=%s&plist="
00054390   "POST %s HTTP/1.1"
000543a2   "Host: %s"
000543ac   "User-Agent: %s"
000543bc   "Accept: text/html"
000543cf   "Connection: Close"
000543e2   "Content-Type: application/x-www-"
00054402   "form-urlencoded"
00054413   "Content-Length: %d"
00054430   "id=%s&data=%s"
00054440   "POST %s HTTP/1.1"
00054452   "Host: %s"
0005445c   "User-Agent: %s"
0005446c   "Accept: text/html"
0005447f   "Connection: Close"
00054492   "Content-Type: application/x-www-"
000544b2   "form-urlencoded"
000544c3   "Content-Length: %d"
000544e0   "GET %s HTTP/1.0"
000544f1   "Host: %s"
000544fb   "User-Agent: %s"
0005450b   "Connection: close"
00054528   "POST /get/scr.html HTTP/1.0"
00054545   "Host: %s"
0005454f   "User-Agent: %s"
0005455f   "Connection: close"
00054572   "Content-Length: %d"
00054586   "Content-Type: multipart/form-dat"
000545a6   "a; boundary=--------------------"
000545c6   "-------%d"
000545d4   "----------------------------%d"
000545f8   "%sContent-Disposition: form-data"
00054618   "; name="id""
00054630   "%sContent-Disposition: form-data"
00054650   "; name="screen"; filename="%d""
00054670   "Content-Type: application/octet-"
00054690   "stream"
000546a0   "%s(%d) : %s"
000546ac   "%s failed with error %d: %s"
000546c8   "%02X"
000546d8   "BlackwoodPRO"
000546e8   "FinamDirect"
000546f4   "GrayBox"
000546fc   "MbtPRO"
00054704   "Laser"
0005470c   "LightSpeed"
00054718   "LTGroup"
00054720   "Mbt"
00054724   "ScotTrader"
00054730   "SaxoTrader"
```

```
00054740  "Program:   %s"
0005474f  "Username:  %s"
0005475e  "Password:  %s"
0005476d  "AccountNO: %s"
0005477c  "Server:    %s"
00054790  "%s %s"
0005479c  "PROCESSOR_IDENTIFIER"
[...]
0005a8e0  "mintrayway.com"
0005aa98  "Mozilla/4.0 (compatible; MSIE 8."
0005aab8  "0; Windows NT 6.0; Trident/4.0; "
0005aad8  "MathPlayer 2.10d; SLCC1; .NET CL"
0005aaf8  "R 2.0.50727; Media Center PC 5.0"
0005ab18  "; .NET CLR 3.5.30729; .NET CLR 3"
0005ab38  ".0.30729)"
[...]

0:012> s-su 00040000 0005d000
[...]
00055004  "\chkntfs.exe"
00055020  "\chkntfs.dat"
[...]
00058e20  "kernel32.dll"
00058e3c  "user32.dll"
00058e54  "ws2_32.dll"
00058e6c  "ntdll.dll"
00058e80  "wininet.dll"
00058e98  "nspr4.dll"
00058eac  "ssl3.dll"
0005a4e0  "C:\Users\dima\AppData\Roaming\ch"
0005a520  "kntfs.dat"
[...]
```

We find some references to **Fake Module** chkntfs.exe here and the list of modules needed for this malware. Such modules such as wininet.dll may be checked for any **Patched Code**.

Let's now check if there are any **Hidden Modules** not shown in loaded module list by using **.imgscan** command that searches for MZ/PE signatures:

```
0:012> .imgscan
MZ at 00040000, prot 00000040, type 00020000 - size 1d000
MZ at 00060000, prot 00000008, type 00040000 - size 3000
MZ at 00850000, prot 00000002, type 01000000 - size 9c000
  Name: iexplore.exe
MZ at 01d40000, prot 00000008, type 00040000 - size b000
MZ at 01d70000, prot 00000008, type 00040000 - size a000
MZ at 01f70000, prot 00000008, type 00040000 - size 12f000
MZ at 021b0000, prot 00000002, type 00040000 - size 2000
MZ at 02200000, prot 00000008, type 00040000 - size a000
MZ at 023e0000, prot 00000008, type 00040000 - size 6000
MZ at 02530000, prot 00000002, type 00040000 - size 2000
MZ at 025a0000, prot 00000002, type 00040000 - size 5000
MZ at 028c0000, prot 00000008, type 00040000 - size 3000
MZ at 02a10000, prot 00000008, type 00040000 - size 3000
MZ at 02b90000, prot 00000008, type 00040000 - size 3000
MZ at 02ba0000, prot 00000008, type 00040000 - size 3000
MZ at 02bc0000, prot 00000008, type 00040000 - size 8000
MZ at 02d10000, prot 00000008, type 00040000 - size 4000
MZ at 038d0000, prot 00000002, type 00040000 - size 191000
```

```
MZ at 03b70000, prot 00000008, type 00040000 - size 3000
MZ at 03b80000, prot 00000008, type 00040000 - size 3000
MZ at 03bd0000, prot 00000008, type 00040000 - size 3000
MZ at 03bf0000, prot 00000008, type 00040000 - size 3000
MZ at 03c00000, prot 00000008, type 00040000 - size 3000
MZ at 04000000, prot 00000008, type 00040000 - size d000
MZ at 044f0000, prot 00000008, type 00040000 - size 5000
MZ at 04870000, prot 00000008, type 00040000 - size 3000
MZ at 04910000, prot 00000008, type 00040000 - size 4000
MZ at 04f00000, prot 00000002, type 01000000 - size 335000
  Name: igdumd32.dll
MZ at 053d0000, prot 00000008, type 00040000 - size b0000
MZ at 05b20000, prot 00000008, type 00040000 - size 7000
MZ at 05fc0000, prot 00000008, type 00040000 - size 89000
MZ at 06050000, prot 00000008, type 00040000 - size 5000
MZ at 096e0000, prot 00000002, type 01000000 - size 21000
  Name: MathMLMimer.dll
MZ at 10000000, prot 00000004, type 00020000 - size 5000
  Name: screens_dll.dll
MZ at 16080000, prot 00000002, type 01000000 - size 25000
  Name: mdnsNSP.dll
MZ at 27500000, prot 00000002, type 01000000 - size 11a000
  Name: msidcrl40.dll
MZ at 29500000, prot 00000002, type 01000000 - size 67000
  Name: IDBHO.DLL
MZ at 633d0000, prot 00000002, type 01000000 - size 4f000
  Name: rpbrowserrecordplugin.dll
MZ at 634b0000, prot 00000002, type 01000000 - size 1d000
  Name: rpchromebrowserrecordhelper.dll
MZ at 63f00000, prot 00000002, type 01000000 - size c000
  Name: mscorie.dll
MZ at 67320000, prot 00000002, type 01000000 - size 5e3000
  Name: Flash.ocx
MZ at 6c170000, prot 00000002, type 01000000 - size 57000
  Name: dxtmsft.dll
MZ at 6c230000, prot 00000002, type 01000000 - size b4000
  Name: JSCRIPT.dll
MZ at 6c460000, prot 00000002, type 01000000 - size cc000
  Name: d3dim700.dll
MZ at 6c640000, prot 00000002, type 01000000 - size 6a000
  Name: VBSCRIPT.dll
MZ at 6c6e0000, prot 00000002, type 01000000 - size 39000
  Name: dxtrans.dll
MZ at 6c830000, prot 00000002, type 01000000 - size 5b0000
  Name: MSHTML.dll
MZ at 6cde0000, prot 00000002, type 01000000 - size a000
  Name: DDRAWEX.DLL
MZ at 6cdf0000, prot 00000002, type 01000000 - size e000
  Name: PNGFILTER.DLL
MZ at 6cfe0000, prot 00000002, type 01000000 - size 29000
  Name: msls31.dll
MZ at 6d230000, prot 00000002, type 01000000 - size b000
  Name: msimtf.dll
MZ at 6d260000, prot 00000002, type 01000000 - size c000
  Name: ImgUtil.dll
MZ at 6d440000, prot 00000002, type 01000000 - size c000
  Name: jp2ssv.dll
MZ at 6dbb0000, prot 00000002, type 01000000 - size 30000
  Name: MLANG.dll
MZ at 6df80000, prot 00000002, type 01000000 - size 1b000
```

```
  Name: CRYPTNET.dll
MZ at 6ec60000, prot 00000002, type 01000000 - size 4a000
  Name: RASAPI32.dll
MZ at 6f040000, prot 00000002, type 01000000 - size 31000
  Name: TAPI32.dll
MZ at 6f0c0000, prot 00000002, type 01000000 - size 136000
  Name: MSXML3.dll
MZ at 6f310000, prot 00000002, type 01000000 - size 6000
  Name: SensApi.dll
MZ at 6f350000, prot 00000002, type 01000000 - size 14000
  Name: rasman.dll
MZ at 6f3b0000, prot 00000002, type 01000000 - size c000
  Name: rtutils.dll
MZ at 6f5a0000, prot 00000002, type 01000000 - size 6000
  Name: rasadhlp.dll
MZ at 6f620000, prot 00000002, type 01000000 - size 70000
  Name: DSOUND.dll
MZ at 6fa10000, prot 00000002, type 01000000 - size 12000
  Name: PNRPNSP.dll
MZ at 6fd00000, prot 00000002, type 01000000 - size 9b000
  Name: MSVCR80.dll
MZ at 6fec0000, prot 00000002, type 01000000 - size e5000
  Name: DDRAW.dll
MZ at 700c0000, prot 00000002, type 01000000 - size a94000
  Name: IEFRAME.dll
MZ at 712a0000, prot 00000002, type 01000000 - size 8000
  Name: WINRNR.dll
MZ at 71300000, prot 00000002, type 01000000 - size 62000
  Name: mscms.dll
MZ at 71390000, prot 00000002, type 01000000 - size 42000
  Name: WINSPOOL.DRV
MZ at 718f0000, prot 00000002, type 01000000 - size 53000
  Name: SWEEPRX.dll
MZ at 72130000, prot 00000002, type 01000000 - size 6000
  Name: DCIMAN32.dll
MZ at 721a0000, prot 00000002, type 01000000 - size 1f000
  Name: EhStorAPI.DLL
MZ at 725d0000, prot 00000002, type 01000000 - size 96000
  Name: fwpuclnt.dll
MZ at 72a30000, prot 00000002, type 01000000 - size c000
  Name: dwmapi.dll
MZ at 73090000, prot 00000002, type 01000000 - size 60000
  Name: tiptsf.dll
MZ at 73100000, prot 00000002, type 01000000 - size 4c000
  Name: Wpc.DLL
MZ at 73150000, prot 00000002, type 01000000 - size 12000
  Name: mp3acm.dll
MZ at 73240000, prot 00000002, type 01000000 - size 4a000
  Name: mscoree.dll
MZ at 73330000, prot 00000002, type 01000000 - size 8000
  Name: MSADP32.dll
MZ at 734e0000, prot 00000002, type 01000000 - size 33000
  Name: IEShims.dll
MZ at 73520000, prot 00000002, type 01000000 - size 9000
  Name: MSGSM32.dll
MZ at 73540000, prot 00000002, type 01000000 - size 8000
  Name: DispEx.dll
MZ at 73600000, prot 00000002, type 01000000 - size 40000
  Name: SWEEPRX.dll
MZ at 73650000, prot 00000002, type 01000000 - size 7000
```

```
  Name: MIDIMAP.dll
MZ at 73660000, prot 00000002, type 01000000 - size 66000
  Name: audioeng.dll
MZ at 736d0000, prot 00000002, type 01000000 - size 21000
  Name: AudioSes.DLL
MZ at 73700000, prot 00000002, type 01000000 - size f4000
  Name: WindowsCodecs.dll
MZ at 73800000, prot 00000002, type 01000000 - size 2f000
  Name: WINMMDRV.dll
MZ at 73880000, prot 00000002, type 01000000 - size 14000
  Name: MSACM32.dll
MZ at 738a0000, prot 00000002, type 01000000 - size 3d000
  Name: OLEACC.dll
MZ at 738e0000, prot 00000002, type 01000000 - size 32000
  Name: WINMM.dll
MZ at 73a10000, prot 00000002, type 01000000 - size bb000
  Name: PROPSYS.dll
MZ at 73b40000, prot 00000002, type 01000000 - size c000
  Name: wshbth.dll
MZ at 73b60000, prot 00000002, type 01000000 - size f000
  Name: NAPINSP.dll
MZ at 73b70000, prot 00000002, type 01000000 - size 8000
  Name: IMAADP32.dll
MZ at 73b90000, prot 00000002, type 01000000 - size 7000
  Name: MSG711.dll
MZ at 73ba0000, prot 00000002, type 01000000 - size 2f000
  Name: iepeers.DLL
MZ at 73cb0000, prot 00000002, type 01000000 - size 9000
  Name: MSACM32.DRV
MZ at 73d50000, prot 00000002, type 01000000 - size 1ab000
  Name: gdiplus.dll
MZ at 73f00000, prot 00000002, type 01000000 - size 4000
  Name: ksuser.dll
MZ at 743a0000, prot 00000002, type 01000000 - size 19e000
  Name: COMCTL32.dll
MZ at 74550000, prot 00000002, type 01000000 - size 2f000
  Name: XmlLite.dll
MZ at 74580000, prot 00000002, type 01000000 - size 14000
  Name: ATL.DLL
MZ at 74610000, prot 00000002, type 01000000 - size f000
  Name: nlaapi.dll
MZ at 74620000, prot 00000002, type 01000000 - size 15000
  Name: Cabinet.dll
MZ at 74640000, prot 00000002, type 01000000 - size 28000
  Name: MMDevAPI.DLL
MZ at 746a0000, prot 00000002, type 01000000 - size 3f000
  Name: UxTheme.dll
MZ at 747a0000, prot 00000002, type 01000000 - size 2d000
  Name: WINTRUST.dll
MZ at 74860000, prot 00000002, type 01000000 - size a000
  Name: WTSAPI32.dll
MZ at 74870000, prot 00000002, type 01000000 - size 7000
  Name: AVRT.dll
MZ at 74930000, prot 00000002, type 01000000 - size 5000
  Name: WSHTCPIP.dll
MZ at 74940000, prot 00000002, type 01000000 - size 5000
  Name: MSIMG32.dll
MZ at 74950000, prot 00000002, type 01000000 - size 1a000
  Name: POWRPROF.dll
MZ at 74970000, prot 00000002, type 01000000 - size 21000
```

```
  Name: NTMARTA.dll
MZ at 749d0000, prot 00000002, type 01000000 - size 15000
  Name: GPAPI.dll
MZ at 749f0000, prot 00000002, type 01000000 - size 3b000
  Name: RSAENH.dll
MZ at 74a60000, prot 00000002, type 01000000 - size 46000
  Name: SCHANNEL.dll
MZ at 74c70000, prot 00000002, type 01000000 - size 3b000
  Name: MSWSOCK.dll
MZ at 74cd0000, prot 00000002, type 01000000 - size 5000
  Name: WSHIP6.dll
MZ at 74ce0000, prot 00000002, type 01000000 - size 8000
  Name: VERSION.dll
MZ at 74db0000, prot 00000002, type 01000000 - size 45000
  Name: bcrypt.dll
MZ at 74e00000, prot 00000002, type 01000000 - size 7000
  Name: CREDSSP.dll
MZ at 74e10000, prot 00000002, type 01000000 - size 35000
  Name: ncrypt.dll
MZ at 74e60000, prot 00000002, type 01000000 - size 22000
  Name: dhcpcsvc6.DLL
MZ at 74e90000, prot 00000002, type 01000000 - size 7000
  Name: WINNSI.DLL
MZ at 74ea0000, prot 00000002, type 01000000 - size 35000
  Name: dhcpcsvc.DLL
MZ at 74ee0000, prot 00000002, type 01000000 - size 19000
  Name: IPHLPAPI.DLL
MZ at 74f00000, prot 00000002, type 01000000 - size 40000
  Name: wevtapi.dll
MZ at 74f40000, prot 00000002, type 01000000 - size 3a000
  Name: slc.dll
MZ at 74f80000, prot 00000002, type 01000000 - size f2000
  Name: CRYPT32.dll
MZ at 750e0000, prot 00000002, type 01000000 - size 12000
  Name: MSASN1.dll
MZ at 75120000, prot 00000002, type 01000000 - size 11000
  Name: SAMLIB.dll
MZ at 75140000, prot 00000002, type 01000000 - size 76000
  Name: NETAPI32.dll
MZ at 751c0000, prot 00000002, type 01000000 - size 2c000
  Name: DNSAPI.dll
MZ at 75420000, prot 00000002, type 01000000 - size 5f000
  Name: sxs.dll
MZ at 75480000, prot 00000002, type 01000000 - size 2c000
  Name: apphelp.dll
MZ at 754e0000, prot 00000002, type 01000000 - size 14000
  Name: Secur32.dll
MZ at 75500000, prot 00000002, type 01000000 - size 1e000
  Name: USERENV.dll
MZ at 75640000, prot 00000002, type 01000000 - size 7000
  Name: PSAPI.DLL
MZ at 75650000, prot 00000002, type 01000000 - size 9d000
  Name: USER32.dll
MZ at 756f0000, prot 00000002, type 01000000 - size c8000
  Name: MSCTF.dll
MZ at 757c0000, prot 00000002, type 01000000 - size 59000
  Name: SHLWAPI.dll
MZ at 75820000, prot 00000002, type 01000000 - size b10000
  Name: SHELL32.dll
MZ at 76330000, prot 00000002, type 01000000 - size 1e8000
```

```
  Name: iertutil.dll
MZ at 76520000, prot 00000002, type 01000000 - size 2d000
  Name: WS2_32.dll
MZ at 76550000, prot 00000002, type 01000000 - size 73000
  Name: COMDLG32.dll
MZ at 765d0000, prot 00000002, type 01000000 - size aa000
  Name: msvcrt.dll
MZ at 76680000, prot 00000002, type 01000000 - size 7d000
  Name: USP10.dll
MZ at 76700000, prot 00000002, type 01000000 - size e6000
  Name: WININET.dll
MZ at 767f0000, prot 00000002, type 01000000 - size 84000
  Name: CLBCatQ.DLL
MZ at 76880000, prot 00000002, type 01000000 - size 29000
  Name: imagehlp.dll
MZ at 768b0000, prot 00000002, type 01000000 - size 18a000
  Name: SETUPAPI.dll
MZ at 76a40000, prot 00000002, type 01000000 - size 4b000
  Name: GDI32.dll
MZ at 76a90000, prot 00000002, type 01000000 - size c6000
  Name: ADVAPI32.dll
MZ at 76b60000, prot 00000002, type 01000000 - size c3000
  Name: RPCRT4.dll
MZ at 76c30000, prot 00000002, type 01000000 - size 8d000
  Name: OLEAUT32.dll
MZ at 76cc0000, prot 00000002, type 01000000 - size 49000
  Name: WLDAP32.dll
MZ at 76d10000, prot 00000002, type 01000000 - size 133000
  Name: urlmon.dll
MZ at 76e50000, prot 00000002, type 01000000 - size 145000
  Name: ole32.dll
MZ at 76fa0000, prot 00000002, type 01000000 - size 127000
  Name: ntdll.dll
MZ at 770d0000, prot 00000002, type 01000000 - size 6000
  Name: NSI.dll
MZ at 770e0000, prot 00000002, type 01000000 - size 9000
  Name: LPK.dll
MZ at 770f0000, prot 00000002, type 01000000 - size 1e000
  Name: IMM32.dll
MZ at 77110000, prot 00000002, type 01000000 - size dc000
  Name: KERNEL32.dll
MZ at 771f0000, prot 00000002, type 01000000 - size 3000
  Name: Normaliz.dll
MZ at 7c340000, prot 00000002, type 01000000 - size 56000
  Name: MSVCR71.dll
MZ at 7c3a0000, prot 00000002, type 01000000 - size 7b000
  Name: MSVCP71.dll
```

We see *screens_dll.dll* module with read/write protection attribute different from all other found modules:

```
0:012> !address 10000000


Usage:                  <unknown>
Base Address:           10000000
End Address:            10001000
Region Size:            00001000
State:                  00001000 MEM_COMMIT
Protect:                00000004 PAGE_READWRITE
Type:                   00020000 MEM_PRIVATE
Allocation Base:        10000000
Allocation Protect:     00000004 PAGE_READWRITE
```

We now check module headers for this DLL:

```
0:012> !dh 10000000


File Type: DLL
FILE HEADER VALUES
     14C machine (i386)
       4 number of sections
4C8FEE9E time date stamp Tue Sep 14 22:52:30 2010

       0 file pointer to symbol table
       0 number of symbols
      E0 size of optional header
    2102 characteristics
            Executable
            32 bit word machine
            DLL

OPTIONAL HEADER VALUES
     10B magic #
    9.00 linker version
     400 size of code
     800 size of initialized data
       0 size of uninitialized data
    12F3 address of entry point
    1000 base of code
         ----- new -----
10000000 image base
    1000 section alignment
     200 file alignment
       2 subsystem (Windows GUI)
    5.00 operating system version
    0.00 image version
    5.00 subsystem version
    5000 size of image
     400 size of headers
       0 checksum
00100000 size of stack reserve
00001000 size of stack commit
00100000 size of heap reserve
00001000 size of heap commit
     140  DLL characteristics
            Dynamic base
            NX compatible
```

65

```
2330 [       50] address [size] of Export Directory
20E0 [       78] address [size] of Import Directory
   0 [        0] address [size] of Resource Directory
   0 [        0] address [size] of Exception Directory
   0 [        0] address [size] of Security Directory
4000 [       34] address [size] of Base Relocation Directory
2060 [       1C] address [size] of Debug Directory
   0 [        0] address [size] of Description Directory
   0 [        0] address [size] of Special Directory
   0 [        0] address [size] of Thread Storage Directory
   0 [        0] address [size] of Load Configuration Directory
   0 [        0] address [size] of Bound Import Directory
2000 [       58] address [size] of Import Address Table Directory
   0 [        0] address [size] of Delay Import Directory
   0 [        0] address [size] of COR20 Header Directory
   0 [        0] address [size] of Reserved Directory


SECTION HEADER #1
   .text name
10001000 virtual size
    1000 virtual address
     400 size of raw data
     400 file pointer to raw data
       0 file pointer to relocation table
       0 file pointer to line numbers
       0 number of relocations
       0 number of line numbers
60000020 flags
         Code
         (no align specified)
         Execute Read

SECTION HEADER #2
   .rdata name
10002000 virtual size
    2000 virtual address
     400 size of raw data
     800 file pointer to raw data
       0 file pointer to relocation table
       0 file pointer to line numbers
       0 number of relocations
       0 number of line numbers
40000040 flags
         Initialized Data
         (no align specified)
         Read Only


Debug Directories(1)
     Type      Size    Address  Pointer
      cv        46      2094      894    Format: RSDS, guid, 1,
C:\MyWork\screens_dll\Release\screens_dll.pdb

SECTION HEADER #3
   .data name
10003000 virtual size
    3000 virtual address
       0 size of raw data
       0 file pointer to raw data
```

```
          0 file pointer to relocation table
          0 file pointer to line numbers
          0 number of relocations
          0 number of line numbers
C0000040 flags
          Initialized Data
          (no align specified)
          Read Write

SECTION HEADER #4
   .reloc name
10004000 virtual size
    4000 virtual address
     200 size of raw data
     C00 file pointer to raw data
       0 file pointer to relocation table
       0 file pointer to line numbers
       0 number of relocations
       0 number of line numbers
42000040 flags
          Initialized Data
          Discardable
          (no align specified)
          Read Only
```

It looks like a normal DLL but its import address table reveals its purpose (**Namespace**) - screen capture:

```
0:012> dps 10000000+2000 L58/4
10002000  773b6101 gdi32!CreateCompatibleDC
10002004  773b93d6 gdi32!StretchBlt
10002008  773b7461 gdi32!CreateDIBSection
1000200c  773b62a0 gdi32!SelectObject
10002010  00000000
10002014  7627a411 kernel32!lstrcmpW
10002018  762740aa kernel32!VirtualFree
1000201c  7627ad55 kernel32!VirtualAlloc
10002020  00000000
10002024  77419ced user32!ReleaseDC
10002028  77413ba7 user32!NtUserGetWindowDC
1000202c  77420e21 user32!GetWindowRect
10002030  00000000
10002034  745975e9 GdiPlus!GdiplusStartup
10002038  745876dd GdiPlus!GdipSaveImageToStream
1000203c  745bdd38 GdiPlus!GdipGetImageEncodersSize
10002040  745871cf GdiPlus!GdipDisposeImage
10002044  74598591 GdiPlus!GdipCreateBitmapFromHBITMAP
10002048  745bdbae GdiPlus!GdipGetImageEncoders
1000204c  00000000
10002050  7613d51b ole32!CreateStreamOnHGlobal
10002054  00000000
```

We should also check for any patched module code in all modules to which we have matching file binary access:

```
0:012> !for_each_module "!chkimg -d @#ModuleName"

[...]

    77004dba-77004dbd  4 bytes - ntdll!ZwQueryDirectoryFile+6
       [ 00 03 fe 7f:e8 af 05 00 ]
    770051ba-770051bd  4 bytes - ntdll!ZwResumeThread+6 (+0x400)
       [ 00 03 fe 7f:d8 af 05 00 ]
8 errors : ntdll (77004dba-770051bd)

[...]
```

The two reported NTDLL addresses are suspicious as they do not belong to IE (**Out-of-Module Pointer**) and show "garbage":

```
0:012> u 77814dba
ntdll!ZwQueryDirectoryFile+0x6:
77814dba e8af0500ff      call    shell32!MetadataLayout::UpdateDesiredSize+0x218 (7681536e)
77814dbf 12c2            adc     al,dl
77814dc1 2c00            sub     al,0
77814dc3 90              nop
ntdll!NtQueryDirectoryObject:
77814dc4 b8db000000      mov     eax,0DBh
77814dc9 ba0003fe7f      mov     edx,offset SharedUserData!SystemCallStub (7ffe0300)
77814dce ff12            call    dword ptr [edx]
77814dd0 c21c00          ret     1Ch

0:012> u 7681536e
shell32!MetadataLayout::UpdateDesiredSize+0x218:
7681536e 46              inc     esi
7681536f 18894df80f82    sbb     byte ptr [ecx-7DF007B3h],cl
76815375 51              push    ecx
76815376 ff              ???
76815377 ff              ???
76815378 ff8b46288b55    dec     dword ptr [ebx+558B2846h]
7681537e 108d04988b08    adc     byte ptr [ebp+88B9804h],cl
76815384 014df0          add     dword ptr [ebp-10h],ecx

0:004> ub 77814dba
                ^ Unable to find valid previous instruction for 'ub 77814dba'
```

Here we needed to check the beginning of the function because the patching may be done for the part of an instruction such as changing its address or offset:

```
0:012> u ntdll!ZwQueryDirectoryFile
ntdll!ZwQueryDirectoryFile:
77814db4 b8da000000      mov     eax,0DAh
77814db9 bae8af0500      mov     edx,5AFE8h
77814dbe ff12            call    dword ptr [edx]
77814dc0 c22c00          ret     2Ch
77814dc3 90              nop
ntdll!NtQueryDirectoryObject:
77814dc4 b8db000000      mov     eax,0DBh
77814dc9 ba0003fe7f      mov     edx,offset SharedUserData!SystemCallStub (7ffe0300)
77814dce ff12            call    dword ptr [edx]
```

68

Note that a pointer to an indirect call has changed. In the normal case we see this:

```
0:012> dps 7ffe0300 L1
7ffe0300  77815e70 ntdll!KiFastSystemCall
```

In the abnormal case we have execution diversion to already discovered malware module:

```
0:012> dps 5AFE8h L1
0005afe8  0004efe0

0:012> u 0004efe0
0004efe0 58               pop     eax
0004efe1 8d0510ec0400     lea     eax,ds:[4EC10h]
0004efe7 ffe0             jmp     eax
0004efe9 c3               ret
0004efea cc               int     3
0004efeb cc               int     3
0004efec cc               int     3
0004efed cc               int     3

0:012> u 4EC10h
0004ec10 55               push    ebp
0004ec11 8bec             mov     ebp,esp
0004ec13 83ec38           sub     esp,38h
0004ec16 0fb64530         movzx   eax,byte ptr [ebp+30h]
0004ec1a 50               push    eax
0004ec1b 8b4d2c           mov     ecx,dword ptr [ebp+2Ch]
0004ec1e 51               push    ecx
0004ec1f 0fb65528         movzx   edx,byte ptr [ebp+28h]

0:012> !address 4EC10

Usage:                <unknown>
Base Address:         00040000
End Address:          0005d000
Region Size:          0001d000
State:                00001000 MEM_COMMIT
Protect:              00000040 PAGE_EXECUTE_READWRITE
Type:                 00020000 MEM_PRIVATE
Allocation Base:      00040000
Allocation Protect:   00000040 PAGE_EXECUTE_READWRITE
```

Example C

Pattern correspondence

- ⊙ Process Dump
- ⊙ Physical (Complete) Dump
- ⊙ Kernel Dump

© 2014 Software Diagnostics Institute

Many patterns from the two previous examples are applicable for complete memory dumps too. But we need to switch to the appropriate process context. Some patterns are applicable to kernel only memory dumps but will need different commands.

Imagine that instead of IE process memory dump a complete memory dump was generated. We could have been able to use the same commands to detect patterns. In this example we show how to find IE process to check similar information. The complete memory dump is taken from Advanced Windows Memory Dump Analysis training course.

We load a complete memory dump. It has lots of warnings due to the absence of symbols.

```
Microsoft (R) Windows Debugger Version 6.3.9600.16384 AMD64
Copyright (c) Microsoft Corporation. All rights reserved.


Loading Dump File [E:\AdvWMDA-Dumps\64-bit\Complete\MEMORY-Normal.DMP]
Kernel Complete Dump File: Full address space is available

Symbol search path is: *** Invalid ***
************************************************************************
* Symbol loading may be unreliable without a symbol search path.       *
* Use .symfix to have the debugger choose a symbol path.               *
* After setting your symbol path, use .reload to refresh symbol locations. *
************************************************************************
Executable search path is:
************************************************************************
* Symbols can not be loaded because symbol path is not initialized. *
*                                                                   *
* The Symbol Path can be set by:                                    *
*    using the _NT_SYMBOL_PATH environment variable.                *
*    using the -y <symbol_path> argument when starting the debugger. *
*    using .sympath and .sympath+                                   *
************************************************************************
*** ERROR: Symbol file could not be found.  Defaulted to export symbols for ntkrnlmp.exe -
Windows Vista Kernel Version 6000 MP (2 procs) Free x64
Product: WinNt, suite: TerminalServer SingleUserTS Personal
Built by: 6000.16386.amd64fre.vista_rtm.061101-2205
Machine Name:
Kernel base = 0xfffff800`01800000 PsLoadedModuleList = 0xfffff800`01999e90
Debug session time: Tue Jul 12 17:18:12.325 2011 (UTC + 1:00)
System Uptime: 0 days 0:11:03.409
************************************************************************
* Symbols can not be loaded because symbol path is not initialized. *
*                                                                   *
* The Symbol Path can be set by:                                    *
*    using the _NT_SYMBOL_PATH environment variable.                *
*    using the -y <symbol_path> argument when starting the debugger. *
*    using .sympath and .sympath+                                   *
************************************************************************
*** ERROR: Symbol file could not be found.  Defaulted to export symbols for ntkrnlmp.exe -
Loading Kernel Symbols
...........................................................
...........................................................
.........
Loading User Symbols
................
Loading unloaded module list
.........*** ERROR: Symbol file could not be found.  Defaulted to export symbols for ntdll.dll
-
```

```
************* Symbol Loading Error Summary **************
Module name          Error
ntkrnlmp             The system cannot find the file specified
ntdll                The system cannot find the file specified

You can troubleshoot most symbol related issues by turning on symbol loading diagnostics (!sym
noisy) and repeating the command that caused symbols to be loaded.
You should also verify that your symbol search path (.sympath) is correct.
*************************************************************************
*                                                                       *
*                      Bugcheck Analysis                                *
*                                                                       *
*************************************************************************

Use !analyze -v to get detailed debugging information.

BugCheck D1, {fffff88002c04800, 2, 0, fffff9800e6e117a}

*** ERROR: Module load completed but symbols could not be loaded for myfault.sys
*** ERROR: Symbol file could not be found.  Defaulted to export symbols for kernel32.dll -
*** ERROR: Symbol file could not be found.  Defaulted to export symbols for USER32.dll -
***** Kernel symbols are WRONG. Please fix symbols to do analysis.

*************************************************************************
***                                                                  ***
***                                                                  ***
***      Either you specified an unqualified symbol, or your debugger ***
***      doesn't have full symbol information.  Unqualified symbol   ***
***      resolution is turned off by default. Please either specify a ***
***      fully qualified symbol module!symbolname, or enable resolution ***
***      of unqualified symbols by typing ".symopt- 100". Note that  ***
***      enabling unqualified symbol resolution with network symbol  ***
***      server shares in the symbol path may cause the debugger to  ***
***      appear to hang for long periods of time when an incorrect   ***
***      symbol name is typed or the network symbol server is down.  ***
***                                                                  ***
***      For some commands to work properly, your symbol path        ***
***      must point to .pdb files that have full type information.   ***
***                                                                  ***
***      Certain .pdb files (such as the public OS symbols) do not   ***
***      contain the required information.  Contact the group that   ***
***      provided you with these symbols if you need this command to ***
***      work.                                                       ***
***                                                                  ***
***      Type referenced: nt!_KPRCB                                  ***
***                                                                  ***
*************************************************************************
*************************************************************************
***                                                                  ***
***                                                                  ***
***      Either you specified an unqualified symbol, or your debugger ***
***      doesn't have full symbol information.  Unqualified symbol   ***
***      resolution is turned off by default. Please either specify a ***
***      fully qualified symbol module!symbolname, or enable resolution ***
***      of unqualified symbols by typing ".symopt- 100". Note that  ***
***      enabling unqualified symbol resolution with network symbol  ***
***      server shares in the symbol path may cause the debugger to  ***
***      appear to hang for long periods of time when an incorrect   ***
***      symbol name is typed or the network symbol server is down.  ***
***                                                                  ***
```

```
***     For some commands to work properly, your symbol path        ***
***     must point to .pdb files that have full type information.    ***
***                                                                  ***
***     Certain .pdb files (such as the public OS symbols) do not    ***
***     contain the required information.  Contact the group that    ***
***     provided you with these symbols if you need this command to  ***
***     work.                                                        ***
***                                                                  ***
***     Type referenced: nt!KPRCB                                    ***
***                                                                  ***
********************************************************************************
********************************************************************************
***                                                                  ***
***                                                                  ***
***     Either you specified an unqualified symbol, or your debugger ***
***     doesn't have full symbol information.  Unqualified symbol    ***
***     resolution is turned off by default. Please either specify a ***
***     fully qualified symbol module!symbolname, or enable resolution ***
***     of unqualified symbols by typing ".symopt- 100". Note that   ***
***     enabling unqualified symbol resolution with network symbol   ***
***     server shares in the symbol path may cause the debugger to   ***
***     appear to hang for long periods of time when an incorrect    ***
***     symbol name is typed or the network symbol server is down.   ***
***                                                                  ***
***     For some commands to work properly, your symbol path         ***
***     must point to .pdb files that have full type information.     ***
***                                                                  ***
***     Certain .pdb files (such as the public OS symbols) do not     ***
***     contain the required information.  Contact the group that     ***
***     provided you with these symbols if you need this command to   ***
***     work.                                                         ***
***                                                                  ***
***     Type referenced: nt!_KPRCB                                    ***
***                                                                  ***
********************************************************************************
********************************************************************************
***                                                                  ***
***                                                                  ***
***     Either you specified an unqualified symbol, or your debugger ***
***     doesn't have full symbol information.  Unqualified symbol    ***
***     resolution is turned off by default. Please either specify a ***
***     fully qualified symbol module!symbolname, or enable resolution ***
***     of unqualified symbols by typing ".symopt- 100". Note that   ***
***     enabling unqualified symbol resolution with network symbol   ***
***     server shares in the symbol path may cause the debugger to   ***
***     appear to hang for long periods of time when an incorrect    ***
***     symbol name is typed or the network symbol server is down.   ***
***                                                                  ***
***     For some commands to work properly, your symbol path         ***
***     must point to .pdb files that have full type information.     ***
***                                                                  ***
***     Certain .pdb files (such as the public OS symbols) do not     ***
***     contain the required information.  Contact the group that     ***
***     provided you with these symbols if you need this command to   ***
***     work.                                                         ***
***                                                                  ***
***     Type referenced: nt!KPRCB                                    ***
***                                                                  ***
********************************************************************************
********************************************************************************
```

```
***                                                                    ***
***                                                                    ***
***      Either you specified an unqualified symbol, or your debugger  ***
***      doesn't have full symbol information.  Unqualified symbol     ***
***      resolution is turned off by default. Please either specify a  ***
***      fully qualified symbol module!symbolname, or enable resolution ***
***      of unqualified symbols by typing ".symopt- 100". Note that    ***
***      enabling unqualified symbol resolution with network symbol    ***
***      server shares in the symbol path may cause the debugger to    ***
***      appear to hang for long periods of time when an incorrect     ***
***      symbol name is typed or the network symbol server is down.    ***
***                                                                    ***
***      For some commands to work properly, your symbol path          ***
***      must point to .pdb files that have full type information.     ***
***                                                                    ***
***      Certain .pdb files (such as the public OS symbols) do not     ***
***      contain the required information.  Contact the group that     ***
***      provided you with these symbols if you need this command to   ***
***      work.                                                         ***
***                                                                    ***
***      Type referenced: nt!_KPRCB                                    ***
***                                                                    ***
************************************************************************
************************************************************************
***                                                                    ***
***                                                                    ***
***      Either you specified an unqualified symbol, or your debugger  ***
***      doesn't have full symbol information.  Unqualified symbol     ***
***      resolution is turned off by default. Please either specify a  ***
***      fully qualified symbol module!symbolname, or enable resolution ***
***      of unqualified symbols by typing ".symopt- 100". Note that    ***
***      enabling unqualified symbol resolution with network symbol    ***
***      server shares in the symbol path may cause the debugger to    ***
***      appear to hang for long periods of time when an incorrect     ***
***      symbol name is typed or the network symbol server is down.    ***
***                                                                    ***
***      For some commands to work properly, your symbol path          ***
***      must point to .pdb files that have full type information.     ***
***                                                                    ***
***      Certain .pdb files (such as the public OS symbols) do not     ***
***      contain the required information.  Contact the group that     ***
***      provided you with these symbols if you need this command to   ***
***      work.                                                         ***
***                                                                    ***
***      Type referenced: nt!_KPRCB                                    ***
***                                                                    ***
************************************************************************
************************************************************************
***                                                                    ***
***                                                                    ***
***      Either you specified an unqualified symbol, or your debugger  ***
***      doesn't have full symbol information.  Unqualified symbol     ***
***      resolution is turned off by default. Please either specify a  ***
***      fully qualified symbol module!symbolname, or enable resolution ***
***      of unqualified symbols by typing ".symopt- 100". Note that    ***
***      enabling unqualified symbol resolution with network symbol    ***
***      server shares in the symbol path may cause the debugger to    ***
***      appear to hang for long periods of time when an incorrect     ***
***      symbol name is typed or the network symbol server is down.    ***
***                                                                    ***
```

```
***     For some commands to work properly, your symbol path     ***
***     must point to .pdb files that have full type information. ***
***                                                               ***
***     Certain .pdb files (such as the public OS symbols) do not ***
***     contain the required information.  Contact the group that ***
***     provided you with these symbols if you need this command to ***
***     work.                                                     ***
***                                                               ***
***     Type referenced: nt!_KPRCB                                ***
***                                                               ***
*******************************************************************
*******************************************************************
***                                                               ***
***                                                               ***
***     Either you specified an unqualified symbol, or your debugger ***
***     doesn't have full symbol information.  Unqualified symbol ***
***     resolution is turned off by default. Please either specify a ***
***     fully qualified symbol module!symbolname, or enable resolution ***
***     of unqualified symbols by typing ".symopt- 100". Note that ***
***     enabling unqualified symbol resolution with network symbol ***
***     server shares in the symbol path may cause the debugger to ***
***     appear to hang for long periods of time when an incorrect ***
***     symbol name is typed or the network symbol server is down. ***
***                                                               ***
***     For some commands to work properly, your symbol path     ***
***     must point to .pdb files that have full type information. ***
***                                                               ***
***     Certain .pdb files (such as the public OS symbols) do not ***
***     contain the required information.  Contact the group that ***
***     provided you with these symbols if you need this command to ***
***     work.                                                     ***
***                                                               ***
***     Type referenced: nt!_KPRCB                                ***
***                                                               ***
*******************************************************************
Probably caused by : myfault.sys ( myfault+117a )

Followup: MachineOwner
---------
```

We fix symbols:

```
1: kd> .symfix c:\mss

1: kd> .reload
Loading Kernel Symbols
...........................................................
...........................................................
.........
Loading User Symbols
...............
Loading unloaded module list
.........Unable to enumerate user-mode unloaded modules, NTSTATUS 0xC0000147
```

We check running processes and find IE process:

```
1: kd> !process 0 0
**** NT ACTIVE PROCESS DUMP ****
PROCESS fffffa8000c360b0
    SessionId: none  Cid: 0004    Peb: 00000000  ParentCid: 0000
    DirBase: 00124000  ObjectTable: fffff88000002010  HandleCount: 357.
    Image: System

PROCESS fffffa8002366c10
    SessionId: none  Cid: 0160    Peb: 7fffffdf000  ParentCid: 0004
    DirBase: 2e85c000  ObjectTable: fffff880001310a0  HandleCount:  28.
    Image: smss.exe

PROCESS fffffa80023cba80
    SessionId: 0 Cid: 01a4    Peb: 7fffffd6000  ParentCid: 0198
    DirBase: 263d2000  ObjectTable: fffff880014e74e0  HandleCount: 527.
    Image: csrss.exe

PROCESS fffffa800244dc10
    SessionId: 0 Cid: 01c8    Peb: 7fffffde000  ParentCid: 0198
    DirBase: 25159000  ObjectTable: fffff880015989a0  HandleCount:  99.
    Image: wininit.exe

PROCESS fffffa8002453c10
    SessionId: 1 Cid: 01dc    Peb: 7fffffde000  ParentCid: 01d4
    DirBase: 24c71000  ObjectTable: fffff8800159b610  HandleCount: 356.
    Image: csrss.exe

PROCESS fffffa800245fc10
    SessionId: 1 Cid: 020c    Peb: 7fffffd5000  ParentCid: 01d4
    DirBase: 23778000  ObjectTable: fffff880015acd10  HandleCount: 128.
    Image: winlogon.exe

PROCESS fffffa80024ad920
    SessionId: 0 Cid: 022c    Peb: 7fffffd3000  ParentCid: 01c8
    DirBase: 22d5f000  ObjectTable: fffff880015fc6b0  HandleCount: 232.
    Image: services.exe

PROCESS fffffa80024d7c10
    SessionId: 0 Cid: 0248    Peb: 7fffffdd000  ParentCid: 01c8
    DirBase: 2289e000  ObjectTable: fffff8800162b390  HandleCount: 612.
    Image: lsass.exe

PROCESS fffffa80024dbc10
    SessionId: 0 Cid: 0250    Peb: 7fffffdc000  ParentCid: 01c8
    DirBase: 22a26000  ObjectTable: fffff8800162afa0  HandleCount: 158.
    Image: lsm.exe

PROCESS fffffa800349e9d0
    SessionId: 0 Cid: 02d8    Peb: 7fffffd3000  ParentCid: 022c
    DirBase: 18703000  ObjectTable: fffff880008edae0  HandleCount: 311.
    Image: svchost.exe

PROCESS fffffa800209f880
    SessionId: 0 Cid: 0310    Peb: 7fffffd3000  ParentCid: 022c
    DirBase: 17293000  ObjectTable: fffff88001693ad0  HandleCount: 297.
    Image: svchost.exe
```

```
PROCESS ffffffa8002090c10
    SessionId: 0  Cid: 0330    Peb: 7ffffffd6000  ParentCid: 022c
    DirBase: 156c1000  ObjectTable: ffffff880017d8c00  HandleCount: 320.
    Image: svchost.exe

PROCESS ffffffa8002f10970
    SessionId: 0  Cid: 0398    Peb: 7ffffffd5000  ParentCid: 022c
    DirBase: 12eed000  ObjectTable: ffffff880016c5c80  HandleCount: 394.
    Image: svchost.exe

PROCESS ffffffa80031c54f0
    SessionId: 0  Cid: 03b4    Peb: 7ffffffd7000  ParentCid: 022c
    DirBase: 116b3000  ObjectTable: ffffff88001885580  HandleCount: 386.
    Image: svchost.exe

PROCESS ffffffa8003325540
    SessionId: 0  Cid: 03c8    Peb: 7ffffffd7000  ParentCid: 022c
    DirBase: 10e79000  ObjectTable: ffffff880018b26e0  HandleCount: 1091.
    Image: svchost.exe

PROCESS ffffffa800335f040
    SessionId: 0  Cid: 016c    Peb: 7ffffffda000  ParentCid: 0398
    DirBase: 0d691000  ObjectTable: ffffff8800167f590  HandleCount: 113.
    Image: audiodg.exe

PROCESS ffffffa80033902b0
    SessionId: 0  Cid: 0180    Peb: 7ffffffdc000  ParentCid: 022c
    DirBase: 0b916000  ObjectTable: ffffff8800188c920  HandleCount:  70.
    Image: SLsvc.exe

PROCESS ffffffa8003424ae0
    SessionId: 0  Cid: 0374    Peb: 7ffffffda000  ParentCid: 022c
    DirBase: 0a6ec000  ObjectTable: ffffff8800191b900  HandleCount: 554.
    Image: svchost.exe

PROCESS ffffffa8003475840
    SessionId: 0  Cid: 0428    Peb: 7ffffffda000  ParentCid: 022c
    DirBase: 078b8000  ObjectTable: ffffff88001973f00  HandleCount: 477.
    Image: svchost.exe

PROCESS ffffffa80035db8e0
    SessionId: 0  Cid: 04d0    Peb: 7ffffffdf000  ParentCid: 022c
    DirBase: 07e87000  ObjectTable: ffffff88001986cb0  HandleCount: 329.
    Image: spoolsv.exe

PROCESS ffffffa80035edae0
    SessionId: 0  Cid: 04ec    Peb: 7ffffffd5000  ParentCid: 022c
    DirBase: 07515000  ObjectTable: ffffff88001978ee0  HandleCount: 283.
    Image: svchost.exe

PROCESS ffffffa80038ee9b0
    SessionId: 0  Cid: 0620    Peb: 7ffffffd7000  ParentCid: 022c
    DirBase: 05763000  ObjectTable: ffffff88001a6a870  HandleCount: 107.
    Image: svchost.exe

PROCESS ffffffa800392c2e0
    SessionId: 0  Cid: 0640    Peb: 7ffffffd5000  ParentCid: 022c
    DirBase: 049aa000  ObjectTable: ffffff880009bad80  HandleCount: 242.
    Image: vmtoolsd.exe
```

```
PROCESS ffffa80039a2940
    SessionId: 1 Cid: 0728    Peb: 7ffffd8000  ParentCid: 03b4
    DirBase: 27e56000  ObjectTable: fffff88001b53c40  HandleCount:  92.
    Image: dwm.exe

PROCESS ffffa80039bac10
    SessionId: 1 Cid: 0734    Peb: 7fffffde000  ParentCid: 0720
    DirBase: 2d6c9000  ObjectTable: fffff8800180cec0  HandleCount: 824.
    Image: explorer.exe

PROCESS ffffa80039f5040
    SessionId: 0 Cid: 076c    Peb: 7fffffdf000  ParentCid: 022c
    DirBase: 282cb000  ObjectTable: fffff88001a3b110  HandleCount:  88.
    Image: svchost.exe

PROCESS ffffa80039fd040
    SessionId: 0 Cid: 0780    Peb: 7fffffdd000  ParentCid: 022c
    DirBase: 26e92000  ObjectTable: fffff88001a35dd0  HandleCount: 703.
    Image: SearchIndexer.exe

PROCESS ffffa8003bac760
    SessionId: 0 Cid: 07cc    Peb: 7fffffde000  ParentCid: 022c
    DirBase: 278c7000  ObjectTable: fffff88001bc9fa0  HandleCount:  90.
    Image: VMUpgradeHelper.exe

PROCESS ffffa8003b500a0
    SessionId: 1 Cid: 061c    Peb: 7fffffdf000  ParentCid: 03c8
    DirBase: 0f1ea000  ObjectTable: fffff880018296c0  HandleCount: 302.
    Image: taskeng.exe

PROCESS ffffa8003b9ac10
    SessionId: 0 Cid: 0710    Peb: 7fffffdb000  ParentCid: 022c
    DirBase: 1a50e000  ObjectTable: fffff88001c370b0  HandleCount: 127.
    Image: TPAutoConnSvc.exe

PROCESS ffffa80039f1c10
    SessionId: 0 Cid: 01d8    Peb: 7fffffd9000  ParentCid: 03c8
    DirBase: 20a3c000  ObjectTable: fffff88001cc0710  HandleCount:  84.
    Image: taskeng.exe

PROCESS ffffa8004039040
    SessionId: 1 Cid: 08f4    Peb: 7fffffdb000  ParentCid: 0710
    DirBase: 193d7000  ObjectTable: fffff88001b6e4d0  HandleCount: 125.
    Image: TPAutoConnect.exe

PROCESS ffffa80040a3410
    SessionId: 0 Cid: 093c    Peb: 7fffffdb000  ParentCid: 022c
    DirBase: 16561000  ObjectTable: fffff88001e495d0  HandleCount: 245.
    Image: dllhost.exe

PROCESS ffffa80040fba50
    SessionId: 1 Cid: 09f4    Peb: 7fffffde000  ParentCid: 0734
    DirBase: 0b54f000  ObjectTable: fffff88001ec95c0  HandleCount: 382.
    Image: MSASCui.exe

PROCESS ffffa80040cc280
    SessionId: 1 Cid: 0a00    Peb: 7ffffd3000  ParentCid: 0734
    DirBase: 06bda000  ObjectTable: fffff88001a93920  HandleCount:  67.
    Image: VMwareTray.exe
```

```
PROCESS fffffa80020a1c10
    SessionId: 1  Cid: 0a08    Peb: 7fffffdf000  ParentCid: 0734
    DirBase: 0c19f000  ObjectTable: fffff88001ee97b0  HandleCount: 208.
    Image: VMwareUser.exe

PROCESS fffffa8003994990
    SessionId: 1  Cid: 0a1c    Peb: 7fffffde000  ParentCid: 0734
    DirBase: 1d9ec000  ObjectTable: fffff88001e5f4f0  HandleCount: 428.
    Image: sidebar.exe

PROCESS fffffa80040e1ae0
    SessionId: 0  Cid: 0a2c    Peb: 7fffffd5000  ParentCid: 022c
    DirBase: 1d37b000  ObjectTable: fffff88001814f00  HandleCount: 162.
    Image: msdtc.exe

PROCESS fffffa8001361040
    SessionId: 0  Cid: 09ec    Peb: 7fffffde000  ParentCid: 02d8
    DirBase: 37fa4000  ObjectTable: fffff880018e70b0  HandleCount: 108.
    Image: WmiPrvSE.exe

PROCESS fffffa8001519040
    SessionId: 0  Cid: 08e8    Peb: 7fffffd7000  ParentCid: 02d8
    DirBase: 137c1000  ObjectTable: fffff88002e788d0  HandleCount: 162.
    Image: WmiPrvSE.exe

PROCESS fffffa80014f0040
    SessionId: 1  Cid: 0370    Peb: 7efdf000  ParentCid: 05f0
    DirBase: 1b3d8000  ObjectTable: fffff88001689350  HandleCount: 238.
    Image: ieuser.exe

PROCESS fffffa80040d2040
    SessionId: 1  Cid: 05b0    Peb: 7efdf000  ParentCid: 05f0
    DirBase: 03d42000  ObjectTable: fffff88002740010  HandleCount: 336.
    Image: iexplore.exe

PROCESS fffffa8001571040
    SessionId: 0  Cid: 0590    Peb: 7fffffd4000  ParentCid: 0780
    DirBase: 316ee000  ObjectTable: fffff88002d819f0  HandleCount: 246.
    Image: SearchProtocolHost.exe

PROCESS fffffa80014ce2f0
    SessionId: 0  Cid: 071c    Peb: 7fffffd7000  ParentCid: 0780
    DirBase: 23ab9000  ObjectTable: fffff88002c220b0  HandleCount:  90.
    Image: SearchFilterHost.exe

PROCESS fffffa8001579040
    SessionId: 1  Cid: 0948    Peb: 7fffffde000  ParentCid: 0734
    DirBase: 2863d000  ObjectTable: fffff880017bc580  HandleCount:  48.
    Image: notepad.exe

PROCESS fffffa800159fb40
    SessionId: 1  Cid: 07c8    Peb: 7fffffd7000  ParentCid: 02d8
    DirBase: 3228c000  ObjectTable: fffff8800259fda0  HandleCount:  83.
    Image: dllhost.exe

PROCESS fffffa8001579c10
    SessionId: 0  Cid: 08c8    Peb: 7fffffd9000  ParentCid: 02d8
    DirBase: 1ef31000  ObjectTable: fffff88002702900  HandleCount:  79.
    Image: dllhost.exe
```

```
PROCESS fffffa8001412040
    SessionId: 1  Cid: 03bc    Peb: 7fffffd4000  ParentCid: 0734
    DirBase: 16e27000  ObjectTable: fffff8800327b5e0  HandleCount:  49.
    Image: NotMyfault.exe
```

We check IE process **Stack Trace Collection** (we use 3f flags to have the process context, the correct physical to virtual translation, established during execution of **!process** command and at the same time to load the needed symbol files for user space module address ranges):

```
1: kd> !process fffffa80040d2040 3f
PROCESS fffffa80040d2040
    SessionId: 1  Cid: 05b0    Peb: 7efdf000  ParentCid: 05f0
    DirBase: 03d42000  ObjectTable: fffff88002740010  HandleCount: 336.
    Image: iexplore.exe
    VadRoot fffffa80013f4970 Vads 275 Clone 0 Private 1536. Modified 56. Locked 0.
    DeviceMap fffff88001697690
    Token                             fffff88002dd0a70
    ElapsedTime                       00:00:28.052
    UserTime                          00:00:00.156
    KernelTime                        00:00:00.265
    QuotaPoolUsage[PagedPool]         205248
    QuotaPoolUsage[NonPagedPool]      28032
    Working Set Sizes (now,min,max)  (5635, 50, 345) (22540KB, 200KB, 1380KB)
    PeakWorkingSetSize                5694
    VirtualSize                       113 Mb
    PeakVirtualSize                   128 Mb
    PageFaultCount                    6778
    MemoryPriority                    BACKGROUND
    BasePriority                      8
    CommitCharge                      3462


    PEB at 000000007efdf000
    InheritedAddressSpace:    No
    ReadImageFileExecOptions: No
    BeingDebugged:            No
    ImageBaseAddress:         0000000000e00000
    Ldr                       00000000777af980
    Ldr.Initialized:          Yes
    Ldr.InInitializationOrderModuleList: 00000000000826e0 . 000000000082a40
    Ldr.InLoadOrderModuleList:           00000000000825f0 . 000000000082ba0
    Ldr.InMemoryOrderModuleList:         0000000000082600 . 000000000082bb0
          Base TimeStamp                     Module
        e00000 4549b133 Nov 02 08:49:55 2006 C:\Program Files (x86)\Internet Explorer\iexplore.exe
       776a0000 4549d372 Nov 02 11:16:02 2006 C:\Windows\system32\ntdll.dll
       74fb0000 4549d371 Nov 02 11:16:01 2006 C:\Windows\system32\wow64.dll
       75580000 4549d374 Nov 02 11:16:04 2006 C:\Windows\system32\wow64win.dll
       759e0000 4549d372 Nov 02 11:16:02 2006 C:\Windows\system32\wow64cpu.dll
    SubSystemData:     0000000000000000
    ProcessHeap:       0000000000080000
    ProcessParameters: 0000000000081d00
    CurrentDirectory:  'C:\Windows\system32\'
    WindowTitle:  'C:\Program Files (x86)\Internet Explorer\iexplore.exe'
    ImageFile:    'C:\Program Files (x86)\Internet Explorer\iexplore.exe'
    CommandLine:  '"C:\Program Files (x86)\Internet Explorer\iexplore.exe" '
    DllPath:      'C:\Program Files (x86)\Internet
Explorer;C:\Windows\system32;C:\Windows\system;C:\Windows;.;C:\Program Files\Internet
Explorer;;C:\Windows\system32;C:\Windows;C:\Windows\System32\Wbem'
    Environment:  0000000000081310
       =::=::\
       ALLUSERSPROFILE=C:\ProgramData
       APPDATA=C:\Users\Training\AppData\Roaming
       CommonProgramFiles=C:\Program Files\Common Files
       CommonProgramFiles(x86)=C:\Program Files (x86)\Common Files
       COMPUTERNAME=LH-UZIYU07F029O
       ComSpec=C:\Windows\system32\cmd.exe
       FP_NO_HOST_CHECK=NO
       HKCU_S=\REGISTRY\CUSER\Software
       HKLM_S=\REGISTRY\MACHINE\Software
       HOMEDRIVE=C:
       HOMEPATH=\Users\Training
       LOCALAPPDATA=C:\Users\Training\AppData\Local
       LOGONSERVER=\\LH-UZIYU07F029O
```

```
NUMBER_OF_PROCESSORS=2
OS=Windows_NT
Path=C:\Program Files\Internet Explorer;;C:\Windows\system32;C:\Windows;C:\Windows\System32\Wbem
PATHEXT=.COM;.EXE;.BAT;.CMD;.VBS;.VBE;.JS;.JSE;.WSF;.WSH;.MSC
PROCESSOR_ARCHITECTURE=AMD64
PROCESSOR_IDENTIFIER=EM64T Family 6 Model 15 Stepping 11, GenuineIntel
PROCESSOR_LEVEL=6
PROCESSOR_REVISION=0f0b
ProgramData=C:\ProgramData
ProgramFiles=C:\Program Files
ProgramFiles(x86)=C:\Program Files (x86)
PUBLIC=C:\Users\Public
SESSIONNAME=Console
SystemDrive=C:
SystemRoot=C:\Windows
TEMP=C:\Users\Training\AppData\Local\Temp
TMP=C:\Users\Training\AppData\Local\Temp
USERDOMAIN=LH-UZIYU07F029O
USERNAME=Training
USERPROFILE=C:\Users\Training
windir=C:\Windows


        THREAD fffffa800141dbb0  Cid 05b0.0890  Teb: 000000007efdb000 Win32Thread: fffff900c228d1d0 WAIT:
(UserRequest) UserMode Non-Alertable
            fffffa80040d2490  SynchronizationEvent
            fffffa800121c180  SynchronizationEvent
        Not impersonating
        DeviceMap               fffff88001697690
        Owning Process          fffffa80040d2040        Image:          iexplore.exe
        Attached Process        N/A             Image:          N/A
        Wait Start TickCount    41157           Ticks: 1301 (0:00:00:20.328)
        Context Switch Count    2106            IdealProcessor: 1               LargeStack
        UserTime                00:00:00.359
        KernelTime              00:00:01.375
        Win32 Start Address iexplore!wWinMainCRTStartup (0x0000000000e02d61)
        Stack Init fffff9800db54db0 Current fffff9800db54260
        Base fffff9800db55000 Limit fffff9800db4a000 Call 0
        Priority 10 BasePriority 8 PriorityDecrement 0 IoPriority 2 PagePriority 5
*** ERROR: Module load completed but symbols could not be loaded for myfault.sys
        Child-SP          RetAddr           Call Site
        fffff980`0db542a0 fffff800`0185d695 nt!KiSwapContext+0x84
        fffff980`0db543e0 fffff800`0185ad2f nt!KiSwapThread+0x125
        fffff980`0db54440 fffff800`01ac1813 nt!KeWaitForMultipleObjects+0x703
        fffff980`0db544b0 fffff800`01ba477a nt!ObpWaitForMultipleObjects+0x216
        fffff980`0db54960 fffff800`0184dcf3 nt!NtWaitForMultipleObjects32+0xd9
        fffff980`0db54bb0 00000000`759e373f nt!KiSystemServiceCopyEnd+0x13 (TrapFrame @ fffff980`0db54c20)
        00000000`0022ea18 00000000`74fbabfe wow64cpu!WaitForMultipleObjects32+0x3a
        00000000`0022eac0 00000000`74fba202 wow64!RunCpuSimulation+0xa
        00000000`0022eaf0 00000000`776de23d wow64!Wow64LdrpInitialize+0x492
        00000000`0022f050 00000000`7774e974 ntdll!LdrpInitializeProcess+0x1333
        00000000`0022f2e0 00000000`776ec4ee ntdll! ?? ::FNODOBFM::`string'+0x1d641
        00000000`0022f380 00000000`00000000 ntdll!LdrInitializeThunk+0xe


        THREAD fffffa80015ce800  Cid 05b0.0bd8  Teb: 000000007efd5000 Win32Thread: 0000000000000000 WAIT: (WrQueue)
UserMode Non-Alertable
            fffffa8003421b00  QueueObject
            fffffa80015ce8b8  NotificationTimer
        Not impersonating
        DeviceMap               fffff88001697690
        Owning Process          fffffa80040d2040        Image:          iexplore.exe
        Attached Process        N/A             Image:          N/A
        Wait Start TickCount    40912           Ticks: 1546 (0:00:00:24.156)
        Context Switch Count    64              IdealProcessor: 1
        UserTime                00:00:00.000
        KernelTime              00:00:00.000
        Win32 Start Address 0x0000000076de3242
        Stack Init fffff980133ffdb0 Current fffff980133ff810
        Base fffff98013400000 Limit fffff980133fa000 Call 0
        Priority 8 BasePriority 8 PriorityDecrement 0 IoPriority 2 PagePriority 5
        Child-SP          RetAddr           Call Site
        fffff980`133ff850 fffff800`0185d695 nt!KiSwapContext+0x84
        fffff980`133ff990 fffff800`01868d10 nt!KiSwapThread+0x125
        fffff980`133ff9f0 fffff800`01a94647 nt!KeRemoveQueueEx+0x848
        fffff980`133ffa80 fffff800`01ac1b7d nt!IoRemoveIoCompletion+0x47
        fffff980`133ffb00 fffff800`0184dcf3 nt!NtRemoveIoCompletion+0x13d
```

```
fffff980`133ffbb0 00000000`759e39a2 nt!KiSystemServiceCopyEnd+0x13 (TrapFrame @ fffff980`133ffc20)
00000000`0110ef18 00000000`74fbabfe wow64cpu!RemoveIoCompletionFault+0x41
00000000`0110eff0 00000000`74fba202 wow64!RunCpuSimulation+0xa
00000000`0110f020 00000000`776c894c wow64!Wow64LdrpInitialize+0x492
00000000`0110f580 00000000`776ec4ee ntdll! ?? ::FNODOBFM::`string'+0x1d777
00000000`0110f620 00000000`00000000 ntdll!LdrInitializeThunk+0xe


        THREAD fffffa80017dfbb0  Cid 05b0.012c  Teb: 000000007efad000 Win32Thread: 0000000000000000 WAIT:
(UserRequest) UserMode Alertable
        fffffa80015b4d10  SynchronizationTimer
        fffffa800128c100  SynchronizationEvent
        Not impersonating
        DeviceMap                 fffff88001697690
        Owning Process            fffffa80040d2040     Image:          iexplore.exe
        Attached Process          N/A          Image:          N/A
        Wait Start TickCount      40710        Ticks: 1748 (0:00:00:27.312)
        Context Switch Count      1            IdealProcessor: 0
        UserTime                  00:00:00.000
        KernelTime                00:00:00.000
        Win32 Start Address 0x0000000077916235
        Stack Init fffff980049b2db0 Current fffff980049b2260
        Base fffff980049b3000 Limit fffff980049ad000 Call 0
        Priority 8 BasePriority 8 PriorityDecrement 0 IoPriority 2 PagePriority 5
        Child-SP          RetAddr           Call Site
        fffff980`049b22a0 fffff800`0185d695 nt!KiSwapContext+0x84
        fffff980`049b23e0 fffff800`0185ad2f nt!KiSwapThread+0x125
        fffff980`049b2440 fffff800`01ac1813 nt!KeWaitForMultipleObjects+0x703
        fffff980`049b24b0 fffff800`01ba477a nt!ObpWaitForMultipleObjects+0x216
        fffff980`049b2960 fffff800`0184dcf3 nt!NtWaitForMultipleObjects32+0xd9
        fffff980`049b2bb0 00000000`759e373f nt!KiSystemServiceCopyEnd+0x13 (TrapFrame @ fffff980`049b2c20)
        00000000`02a9ecc8 00000000`74fbabfe wow64cpu!WaitForMultipleObjects32+0x3a
        00000000`02a9ed70 00000000`74fba202 wow64!RunCpuSimulation+0xa
        00000000`02a9eda0 00000000`776c894c wow64!Wow64LdrpInitialize+0x492
        00000000`02a9f300 00000000`776ec4ee ntdll! ?? ::FNODOBFM::`string'+0x1d777
        00000000`02a9f3a0 00000000`00000000 ntdll!LdrInitializeThunk+0xe


        THREAD fffffa800155ebb0  Cid 05b0.0ab4  Teb: 000000007efaa000 Win32Thread: 0000000000000000 WAIT:
(DelayExecution) UserMode Non-Alertable
        fffffa800155ec68  NotificationTimer
        Not impersonating
        DeviceMap                 fffff88001697690
        Owning Process            fffffa80040d2040     Image:          iexplore.exe
        Attached Process          N/A          Image:          N/A
        Wait Start TickCount      40716        Ticks: 1742 (0:00:00:27.218)
        Context Switch Count      6            IdealProcessor: 1
        UserTime                  00:00:00.000
        KernelTime                00:00:00.000
        Win32 Start Address 0x0000000075bffc53
        Stack Init fffff9800e3d2db0 Current fffff9800e3d2990
        Base fffff9800e3d3000 Limit fffff9800e3cd000 Call 0
        Priority 11 BasePriority 8 PriorityDecrement 3 IoPriority 2 PagePriority 5
        Child-SP          RetAddr           Call Site
        fffff980`0e3d29d0 fffff800`0185d695 nt!KiSwapContext+0x84
        fffff980`0e3d2b10 fffff800`0185bbe9 nt!KiSwapThread+0x125
        fffff980`0e3d2b70 fffff800`01a8b1cd nt!KeDelayExecutionThread+0x339
        fffff980`0e3d2bf0 fffff800`0184dcf3 nt!NtDelayExecution+0x5c
        fffff980`0e3d2c20 00000000`759e3cf9 nt!KiSystemServiceCopyEnd+0x13 (TrapFrame @ fffff980`0e3d2c20)
        00000000`00a5ec18 00000000`759e3bad wow64cpu!CpupSyscallStub+0x9
        00000000`00a5ec20 00000000`74fbabfe wow64cpu!Thunk2ArgNSpNSpReloadState+0x21
        00000000`00a5ec90 00000000`74fba202 wow64!RunCpuSimulation+0xa
        00000000`00a5ecc0 00000000`776c894c wow64!Wow64LdrpInitialize+0x492
        00000000`00a5f220 00000000`776ec4ee ntdll! ?? ::FNODOBFM::`string'+0x1d777
        00000000`00a5f2c0 00000000`00000000 ntdll!LdrInitializeThunk+0xe


        THREAD fffffa8001573bb0  Cid 05b0.0998  Teb: 000000007efa7000 Win32Thread: fffff900c220f330 WAIT:
(UserRequest) UserMode Non-Alertable
        fffffa8003939660  SynchronizationEvent
        fffffa8001521be0  SynchronizationEvent
        Not impersonating
        DeviceMap                 fffff88001697690
        Owning Process            fffffa80040d2040     Image:          iexplore.exe
        Attached Process          N/A          Image:          N/A
        Wait Start TickCount      40917        Ticks: 1541 (0:00:00:24.078)
        Context Switch Count      10           IdealProcessor: 0                LargeStack
        UserTime                  00:00:00.000
        KernelTime                00:00:00.000
```

```
Win32 Start Address 0x0000000076a5639b
Stack Init fffff9801038ddb0 Current fffff9801038d260
Base fffff9801038e000 Limit fffff98010387000 Call 0
Priority 9 BasePriority 8 PriorityDecrement 0 IoPriority 2 PagePriority 5
Child-SP          RetAddr           Call Site
fffff980`1038d2a0 fffff800`0185d695 nt!KiSwapContext+0x84
fffff980`1038d3e0 fffff800`0185ad2f nt!KiSwapThread+0x125
fffff980`1038d440 fffff800`01ac1813 nt!KeWaitForMultipleObjects+0x703
fffff980`1038d4b0 fffff800`01ba477a nt!ObpWaitForMultipleObjects+0x216
fffff980`1038d960 fffff800`0184dcf3 nt!NtWaitForMultipleObjects32+0xd9
fffff980`1038dbb0 00000000`759e373f nt!KiSystemServiceCopyEnd+0x13 (TrapFrame @ fffff980`1038dc20)
00000000`0327ebf8 00000000`74fbabfe wow64cpu!WaitForMultipleObjects32+0x3a
00000000`0327eca0 00000000`74fba202 wow64!RunCpuSimulation+0xa
00000000`0327ecd0 00000000`776c894c wow64!Wow64LdrpInitialize+0x492
00000000`0327f230 00000000`776ec4ee ntdll! ?? ::FNODOBFM::`string'+0x1d777
00000000`0327f2d0 00000000`00000000 ntdll!LdrInitializeThunk+0xe

    THREAD fffffa8001565bb0  Cid 05b0.06c8  Teb: 000000007efa4000 Win32Thread: fffff900c3239b20 WAIT:
(WrUserRequest) UserMode Non-Alertable
        fffffa8003b49950   SynchronizationEvent
    Not impersonating
    DeviceMap                   fffff88001697690
    Owning Process              fffffa80040d2040      Image:         iexplore.exe
    Attached Process            N/A            Image:        N/A
    Wait Start TickCount        41157          Ticks: 1301 (0:00:00:20.328)
    Context Switch Count        1321           IdealProcessor: 1                LargeStack
    UserTime                    00:00:00.296
    KernelTime                  00:00:00.921
    Win32 Start Address 0x000000007306e3a4
    Stack Init fffff98015af5db0 Current fffff98015af58c0
    Base fffff98015af6000 Limit fffff98015aec000 Call 0
    Priority 12 BasePriority 8 PriorityDecrement 2 IoPriority 2 PagePriority 5

    Child-SP          RetAddr           Call Site
    fffff980`15af5900 fffff800`0185d695 nt!KiSwapContext+0x84
    fffff980`15af5a40 fffff800`0185d3dd nt!KiSwapThread+0x125
    fffff980`15af5aa0 fffff960`000c95f8 nt!KeWaitForSingleObject+0x5f5
    fffff980`15af5b20 fffff960`000c9686 win32k!xxxRealSleepThread+0x278
    fffff980`15af5bc0 fffff960`000dbf57 win32k!xxxSleepThread+0x56
    fffff980`15af5bf0 fffff800`0184dcf3 win32k!NtUserWaitMessage+0x37
    fffff980`15af5c20 00000000`759e3cf9 nt!KiSystemServiceCopyEnd+0x13 (TrapFrame @ fffff980`15af5c20)
    00000000`0390ee88 00000000`759e3cb5 wow64cpu!CpupSyscallStub+0x9
    00000000`0390ee90 00000000`74fbabfe wow64cpu!Thunk0Arg+0x5
    00000000`0390ef00 00000000`74fba202 wow64!RunCpuSimulation+0xa
    00000000`0390ef30 00000000`776c894c wow64!Wow64LdrpInitialize+0x492
    00000000`0390f490 00000000`776ec4ee ntdll! ?? ::FNODOBFM::`string'+0x1d777
    00000000`0390f530 00000000`00000000 ntdll!LdrInitializeThunk+0xe

    THREAD fffffa80015cbbb0  Cid 05b0.083c  Teb: 000000007efa1000 Win32Thread: 0000000000000000 WAIT:
(UserRequest) UserMode Alertable
        fffffa8004197190   NotificationEvent
        fffffa80015cbc68   NotificationTimer
    IRP List:
        fffffa80015b8010: (0006,01f0) Flags: 00060070  Mdl: 00000000
    Not impersonating
    DeviceMap                   fffff88001697690
    Owning Process              fffffa80040d2040      Image:         iexplore.exe
    Attached Process            N/A            Image:        N/A
    Wait Start TickCount        41484          Ticks: 974 (0:00:00:15.218)
    Context Switch Count        12             IdealProcessor: 0
    UserTime                    00:00:00.000
    KernelTime                  00:00:00.031
    Win32 Start Address 0x0000000076c22a6b
    Stack Init fffff9800df1cdb0 Current fffff9800df1c960
    Base fffff9800df1d000 Limit fffff9800df17000 Call 0
    Priority 12 BasePriority 8 PriorityDecrement 2 IoPriority 2 PagePriority 5
    Child-SP          RetAddr           Call Site
    fffff980`0df1c9a0 fffff800`0185d695 nt!KiSwapContext+0x84
    fffff980`0df1cae0 fffff800`0185d3dd nt!KiSwapThread+0x125
    fffff980`0df1cb40 fffff800`01a8b27b nt!KeWaitForSingleObject+0x5f5
    fffff980`0df1cbc0 fffff800`0184dcf3 nt!NtWaitForSingleObject+0x9b
    fffff980`0df1cc20 00000000`759e3cf9 nt!KiSystemServiceCopyEnd+0x13 (TrapFrame @ fffff980`0df1cc20)
    00000000`0370ed28 00000000`759e3af6 wow64cpu!CpupSyscallStub+0x9
    00000000`0370ed30 00000000`74fbabfe wow64cpu!Thunk0ArgReloadState+0x1a
    00000000`0370eda0 00000000`74fba202 wow64!RunCpuSimulation+0xa
    00000000`0370edd0 00000000`776c894c wow64!Wow64LdrpInitialize+0x492
```

```
00000000`0370f330 00000000`776ec4ee ntdll! ?? ::FNODOBFM::`string'+0x1d777
00000000`0370f3d0 00000000`00000000 ntdll!LdrInitializeThunk+0xe

      THREAD ffffffa800159e060  Cid 05b0.0a60  Teb: 000000007ef9b000 Win32Thread: ffffff900c315f2e0 WAIT:
(UserRequest) UserMode Non-Alertable
        ffffffa8003b2aad0  SynchronizationEvent
        ffffffa800159e118  NotificationTimer
      Not impersonating
      DeviceMap                 ffffff88001697690
      Owning Process            ffffffa80040d2040      Image:          iexplore.exe
      Attached Process          N/A          Image:          N/A
      Wait Start TickCount      40919          Ticks: 1539 (0:00:00:24.046)
      Context Switch Count      5              IdealProcessor: 0              LargeStack
      UserTime                  00:00:00.000
      KernelTime                00:00:00.000
      Win32 Start Address 0x000000007230dacf
      Stack Init ffffff98011db3db0 Current ffffff98011db3960
      Base ffffff98011db4000 Limit ffffff98011dad000 Call 0
      Priority 9 BasePriority 8 PriorityDecrement 0 IoPriority 2 PagePriority 5
      Child-SP          RetAddr           Call Site
      ffffff980`11db39a0 ffffff800`0185d695 nt!KiSwapContext+0x84
      ffffff980`11db3ae0 ffffff800`0185d3dd nt!KiSwapThread+0x125
      ffffff980`11db3b40 ffffff800`01a8b27b nt!KeWaitForSingleObject+0x5f5
      ffffff980`11db3bc0 ffffff800`0184dcf3 nt!NtWaitForSingleObject+0x9b
      ffffff980`11db3c20 00000000`759e3cf9 nt!KiSystemServiceCopyEnd+0x13 (TrapFrame @ ffffff980`11db3c20)
      00000000`03c4ea68 00000000`759e3af6 wow64cpu!CpupSyscallStub+0x9
      00000000`03c4ea70 00000000`74fbabfe wow64cpu!Thunk0ArgReloadState+0x1a
      00000000`03c4eae0 00000000`74fba202 wow64!RunCpuSimulation+0xa
      00000000`03c4eb10 00000000`776c894c wow64!Wow64LdrpInitialize+0x492
      00000000`03c4f070 00000000`776ec4ee ntdll! ?? ::FNODOBFM::`string'+0x1d777
      00000000`03c4f110 00000000`00000000 ntdll!LdrInitializeThunk+0xe

      THREAD ffffffa80012b7bb0  Cid 05b0.086c  Teb: 000000007ef98000 Win32Thread: ffffff900c30c7ad0 WAIT:
(UserRequest) UserMode Non-Alertable
        ffffffa80039c6dc0  SynchronizationEvent
        ffffffa80012b7c68  NotificationTimer
      Not impersonating
      DeviceMap                 ffffff88001697690
      Owning Process            ffffffa80040d2040      Image:          iexplore.exe
      Attached Process          N/A          Image:          N/A
      Wait Start TickCount      40954          Ticks: 1504 (0:00:00:23.500)
      Context Switch Count      83             IdealProcessor: 1              LargeStack
      UserTime                  00:00:00.093
      KernelTime                00:00:00.062
      Win32 Start Address 0x000000007230dacf
      Stack Init ffffff98010367db0 Current ffffff98010367960
      Base ffffff98010368000 Limit ffffff98010362000 Call 0
      Priority 8 BasePriority 8 PriorityDecrement 0 IoPriority 2 PagePriority 5
      Child-SP          RetAddr           Call Site
      ffffff980`103679a0 ffffff800`0185d695 nt!KiSwapContext+0x84
      ffffff980`10367ae0 ffffff800`0185d3dd nt!KiSwapThread+0x125
      ffffff980`10367b40 ffffff800`01a8b27b nt!KeWaitForSingleObject+0x5f5
      ffffff980`10367bc0 ffffff800`0184dcf3 nt!NtWaitForSingleObject+0x9b
      ffffff980`10367c20 00000000`759e3cf9 nt!KiSystemServiceCopyEnd+0x13 (TrapFrame @ ffffff980`10367c20)
      00000000`0374e9b8 00000000`759e3af6 wow64cpu!CpupSyscallStub+0x9
      00000000`0374e9c0 00000000`74fbabfe wow64cpu!Thunk0ArgReloadState+0x1a
      00000000`0374ea30 00000000`74fba202 wow64!RunCpuSimulation+0xa
      00000000`0374ea60 00000000`776c894c wow64!Wow64LdrpInitialize+0x492
      00000000`0374efc0 00000000`776ec4ee ntdll! ?? ::FNODOBFM::`string'+0x1d777
      00000000`0374f060 00000000`00000000 ntdll!LdrInitializeThunk+0xe
```

We see WOW64 modules on all thread stack traces (**Virtualized Process**). We need to load WOW64 debugging extension and then to switch to one of the threads in x86 mode. After that we are able to check 32-bit modules, disassemble functions, etc.

```
1: kd> .load wow64exts

1: kd> .thread /w fffffa80012b7bb0
Implicit thread is now fffffa80`012b7bb0
WARNING: WOW context retrieval requires
switching to the thread's process context.
Use .process /p fffffa80`01412040 to switch back.
Implicit process is now fffffa80`040d2040
The context is partially valid. Only x86 user-mode context is available.
x86 context set

1: kd:x86> .reload
Loading Kernel Symbols
...............................................................
...............................................................
.........
Loading User Symbols
.....
Loading unloaded module list
.........Unable to enumerate user-mode unloaded modules, NTSTATUS 0xC0000147
Loading Wow64 Symbols
...............................................................
.....................

1: kd:x86> kv
 *** Stack trace for last set context - .thread/.cxr resets it
ChildEBP         RetAddr          Args to Child
043bf9e0 76af1220 00000550 00000000 043bfa28 ntdll_77850000!NtWaitForSingleObject+0x15 (FPO: [3,0,0])
043bfa50 76af1188 00000550 000927c0 00000000 kernel32!WaitForSingleObjectEx+0xbe (FPO: [Non-Fpo])
043bfa64 7238f57d 00000550 000927c0 722f0000 kernel32!WaitForSingleObject+0x12 (FPO: [Non-Fpo])
043bfa7c 72386c92 00000000 00000000 7230dadc mshtml!CDwnTaskExec::ThreadExec+0x127 (FPO: [0,0,4])
043bfa88 7230dadc 043bfa9c 76b619f1 03d85e88 mshtml!CExecFT::ThreadProc+0x3c (FPO: [0,0,0])
043bfa90 76b619f1 03d85e88 043bfadc 778cd109 mshtml!CExecFT::StaticThreadProc+0xd (FPO: [Non-Fpo])
043bfa9c 778cd109 03d85e88 043bdb05 00000000 kernel32!BaseThreadInitThunk+0xe (FPO: [Non-Fpo])
043bfadc 00000000 7230dacf 03d85e88 00000000 ntdll_77850000!_RtlUserThreadStart+0x23 (FPO: [Non-Fpo])

1: kd:x86> lmtu
start             end               module name
00000000`00e00000 00000000`00e9a000   iexplore   Thu Nov 02 08:49:55 2006 (4549B133)
00000000`722f0000 00000000`7265f000   mshtml     Thu Nov 02 09:42:13 2006 (4549BD75)
00000000`72710000 00000000`72787000   mshtmled   Thu Nov 02 09:42:14 2006 (4549BD76)
00000000`72810000 00000000`72888000   jscript    Thu Nov 02 09:39:46 2006 (4549BCE2)
00000000`72900000 00000000`7290e000   pngfilt    Thu Nov 02 09:43:21 2006 (4549BDB9)
00000000`72910000 00000000`72970000   ieapfltr   Thu Nov 02 09:40:04 2006 (4549BCF4)
00000000`72980000 00000000`72991000   SAMLIB     Thu Nov 02 09:43:04 2006 (4549BDA8)
00000000`729a0000 00000000`729c1000   NTMARTA    Thu Nov 02 09:43:55 2006 (4549BDDB)
00000000`729d0000 00000000`72a87000   PROPSYS    Thu Nov 02 09:42:46 2006 (4549BD96)
00000000`72b10000 00000000`72b6f000   SXS        Thu Nov 02 09:43:46 2006 (4549BDD2)
00000000`72b70000 00000000`72d1a000   gdiplus    Thu Nov 02 09:38:55 2006 (4549BCAF)
00000000`72d20000 00000000`72d49000   msls31     Thu Nov 02 09:42:48 2006 (4549BD98)
00000000`72d50000 00000000`72db0000   tiptsf     Thu Nov 02 09:44:19 2006 (4549BDF3)
00000000`72db0000 00000000`72e62000   WindowsCodecs  Thu Nov 02 09:44:51 2006 (4549BE13)
00000000`72e70000 00000000`72e92000   xmllite    Thu Nov 02 09:44:37 2006 (4549BE05)
00000000`72ea0000 00000000`72ed0000   MLANG      Thu Nov 02 09:40:07 2006 (4549BCF7)
00000000`72ed0000 00000000`72f0b000   mswsock    Thu Nov 02 09:42:01 2006 (4549BD69)
00000000`72f10000 00000000`72f63000   actxprxy   Thu Nov 02 09:39:11 2006 (4549BCBF)
00000000`72f70000 00000000`72f7b000   msimtf     Thu Nov 02 09:42:44 2006 (4549BD94)
00000000`72f80000 00000000`72faf000   IEUI       Thu Nov 02 09:40:14 2006 (4549BCFE)
00000000`72fb0000 00000000`72fc2000   pnrpnsp    Thu Nov 02 09:43:28 2006 (4549BDC0)
00000000`72fd0000 00000000`7359a000   IEFRAME    Thu Nov 02 09:40:08 2006 (4549BCF8)
00000000`735a0000 00000000`735a6000   rasadhlp   Thu Nov 02 09:42:58 2006 (4549BDA2)
00000000`735b0000 00000000`735db000   DNSAPI     Thu Nov 02 09:40:01 2006 (4549BCF1)
00000000`735e0000 00000000`73615000   dhcpcsvc   Thu Nov 02 09:39:18 2006 (4549BCC6)
00000000`73620000 00000000`73665000   schannel   Thu Nov 02 09:43:16 2006 (4549BDB4)
00000000`73670000 00000000`73690000   dhcpcsvc6  Thu Nov 02 09:39:19 2006 (4549BCC7)
00000000`73690000 00000000`736a9000   IPHLPAPI   Thu Nov 02 09:41:19 2006 (4549BD3F)
00000000`736b0000 00000000`736bf000   NLAapi     Thu Nov 02 09:42:03 2006 (4549BD6B)
```

```
00000000`736c0000 00000000`736c7000   credssp    Thu Nov 02 09:40:48 2006 (4549BD20)
00000000`736d0000 00000000`73708000   OLEACC     Thu Nov 02 09:42:43 2006 (4549BD93)
00000000`73710000 00000000`73743000   WINMM      Thu Nov 02 09:45:01 2006 (4549BE1D)
00000000`73750000 00000000`737ba000   NETAPI32   Thu Nov 02 09:41:39 2006 (4549BD53)
00000000`737c0000 00000000`738b1000   CRYPT32    Thu Nov 02 09:40:52 2006 (4549BD24)
00000000`738c0000 00000000`73a54000   comctl32   Thu Nov 02 09:40:25 2006 (4549BD09)
00000000`73a60000 00000000`73a67000   WINNSI     Thu Nov 02 09:45:02 2006 (4549BE1E)
00000000`73a70000 00000000`73a76000   sensapi    Thu Nov 02 09:43:50 2006 (4549BDD6)
00000000`73a80000 00000000`73ab1000   TAPI32     Thu Nov 02 09:43:45 2006 (4549BDD1)
00000000`73ac0000 00000000`73b07000   RASAPI32   Thu Nov 02 09:42:59 2006 (4549BDA3)
00000000`73b10000 00000000`73b90000   UxTheme    Thu Nov 02 09:44:25 2006 (4549BDF9)
00000000`73b90000 00000000`73bc8000   rsaenh     Thu Nov 02 09:43:10 2006 (4549BDAE)
00000000`73bd0000 00000000`73bfd000   WINTRUST   Thu Nov 02 09:45:19 2006 (4549BE2F)
00000000`73c00000 00000000`73c87000   AcLayers   Thu Nov 02 09:38:59 2006 (4549BCB3)
00000000`73c90000 00000000`73ca4000   rasman     Thu Nov 02 09:43:07 2006 (4549BDAB)
00000000`73cb0000 00000000`73cc2000   MSASN1     Thu Nov 02 09:41:21 2006 (4549BD41)
00000000`73cd0000 00000000`73d11000   WINSPOOL   Thu Nov 02 09:45:14 2006 (4549BE2A)
00000000`73d20000 00000000`73d5e000   AcRedir    Thu Nov 02 09:39:04 2006 (4549BCB8)
00000000`74f10000 00000000`74f1c000   rtutils    Thu Nov 02 09:43:22 2006 (4549BDBA)
00000000`74f20000 00000000`74f25000   MSIMG32    Thu Nov 02 09:42:42 2006 (4549BD92)
00000000`74f30000 00000000`74f36000   wship6     Thu Nov 02 09:45:05 2006 (4549BE21)
00000000`74f40000 00000000`74f46000   wshtcpip   Thu Nov 02 09:45:11 2006 (4549BE27)
00000000`74f50000 00000000`74f7c000   apphelp    Thu Nov 02 09:38:55 2006 (4549BCAF)
00000000`74f80000 00000000`74f8f000   napinsp    Thu Nov 02 09:41:15 2006 (4549BD3B)
00000000`74f90000 00000000`74f98000   winrnr     Thu Nov 02 09:45:03 2006 (4549BE1F)
00000000`74fa0000 00000000`74fac000   ImgUtil    Thu Nov 02 09:40:55 2006 (4549BD27)
00000000`74fb0000 00000000`74ff5000   wow64      Thu Nov 02 11:16:01 2006 (4549D371)
00000000`75560000 00000000`7557e000   USERENV    Thu Nov 02 09:44:02 2006 (4549BDE2)
00000000`75580000 00000000`755ca000   wow64win   Thu Nov 02 11:16:04 2006 (4549D374)
00000000`75700000 00000000`75714000   MPR        Thu Nov 02 09:40:36 2006 (4549BD14)
00000000`75720000 00000000`7573e000   ShimEng    Thu Nov 02 09:43:19 2006 (4549BDB7)
00000000`759b0000 00000000`759bf000   iebrshim   Thu Nov 02 09:40:05 2006 (4549BCF5)
00000000`759c0000 00000000`759c8000   VERSION    Thu Nov 02 09:44:04 2006 (4549BDE4)
00000000`759e0000 00000000`759e9000   wow64cpu   Thu Nov 02 11:16:02 2006 (4549D372)
00000000`75a50000 00000000`75ab0000   Secur32    Thu Nov 02 09:44:25 2006 (4549BDF9)
00000000`75ab0000 00000000`75b3c000   OLEAUT32   Thu Nov 02 09:42:45 2006 (4549BD95)
00000000`75bc0000 00000000`75d04000   ole32      Thu Nov 02 09:42:42 2006 (4549BD92)
00000000`75d10000 00000000`75d70000   IMM32      Thu Nov 02 09:44:24 2006 (4549BDF8)
00000000`75d70000 00000000`75d79000   LPK        Thu Nov 02 09:44:24 2006 (4549BDF8)
00000000`75d80000 00000000`7684e000   SHELL32    Thu Nov 02 09:43:16 2006 (4549BDB4)
00000000`76850000 00000000`76879000   imagehlp   Thu Nov 02 09:40:47 2006 (4549BD1F)
00000000`76880000 00000000`768ad000   ws2_32     Thu Nov 02 09:44:46 2006 (4549BE0E)
00000000`768b0000 00000000`768f9000   WLDAP32    Thu Nov 02 09:45:40 2006 (4549BE44)
00000000`76900000 00000000`76a24000   urlmon     Thu Nov 02 09:43:55 2006 (4549BDDB)
00000000`76a30000 00000000`76ada000   msvcrt     Thu Nov 02 09:41:53 2006 (4549BD61)
00000000`76ae0000 00000000`76bf0000   kernel32   Thu Nov 02 09:47:00 2006 (4549BE94)
00000000`76bf0000 00000000`76bf7000   PSAPI      Thu Nov 02 09:42:49 2006 (4549BD99)
00000000`76c00000 00000000`76ccf000   WININET    Thu Nov 02 09:44:57 2006 (4549BE19)
00000000`76cd0000 00000000`76d25000   SHLWAPI    Thu Nov 02 09:43:21 2006 (4549BDB9)
00000000`76dc0000 00000000`76eb0000   RPCRT4     Thu Nov 02 09:44:24 2006 (4549BDF8)
00000000`76eb0000 00000000`76f34000   CLBCatQ    Thu Nov 02 09:39:53 2006 (4549BCE9)
00000000`76f40000 00000000`770c8000   SETUPAPI   Thu Nov 02 09:43:12 2006 (4549BDB0)
00000000`770d0000 00000000`771a0000   USER32     Thu Nov 02 09:44:25 2006 (4549BDF9)
00000000`771a0000 00000000`77230000   GDI32      Thu Nov 02 09:44:24 2006 (4549BDF8)
00000000`77230000 00000000`772ef000   ADVAPI32   Thu Nov 02 09:39:30 2006 (4549BCD2)
00000000`772f0000 00000000`773b7000   MSCTF      Thu Nov 02 09:41:30 2006 (4549BD4A)
00000000`773c0000 00000000`77405000   iertutil   Thu Nov 02 09:40:11 2006 (4549BCFB)
00000000`77410000 00000000`7748d000   USP10      Thu Nov 02 09:44:03 2006 (4549BDE3)
00000000`776a0000 00000000`7781a000   ntdll      Thu Nov 02 11:16:02 2006 (4549D372)
00000000`77820000 00000000`77823000   Normaliz   Thu Nov 02 08:33:06 2006 (4549AD42)
00000000`77830000 00000000`77836000   NSI        Thu Nov 02 09:43:35 2006 (4549BDC7)
00000000`77850000 00000000`779a0000   ntdll_77850000   Thu Nov 02 09:44:24 2006 (4549BDF8)

1: kd:x86> !chkimg -d ntdll_77850000
0 errors : ntdll_77850000
```

```
1: kd:x86> !dh ntdll_77850000

File Type: DLL
FILE HEADER VALUES
     14C machine (i386)
       5 number of sections
4549BDF8 time date stamp Thu Nov 02 09:44:24 2006

       0 file pointer to symbol table
       0 number of symbols
      E0 size of optional header
    2102 characteristics
            Executable
            32 bit word machine
            DLL

OPTIONAL HEADER VALUES
     10B magic #
    8.00 linker version
   BF600 size of code
   57C00 size of initialized data
       0 size of uninitialized data
       0 address of entry point
   10000 base of code
         ----- new -----
0000000077850000 image base
   10000 section alignment
     200 file alignment
       3 subsystem (Windows CUI)
    6.00 operating system version
    6.00 image version
    6.00 subsystem version
  150000 size of image
     400 size of headers
  124F8D checksum
0000000000040000 size of stack reserve
0000000000001000 size of stack commit
0000000000100000 size of heap reserve
0000000000001000 size of heap commit
     140  DLL characteristics
            Dynamic base
            NX compatible
   10008 [     ED50] address [size] of Export Directory
       0 [        0] address [size] of Import Directory
   F0000 [    48BC0] address [size] of Resource Directory
       0 [        0] address [size] of Exception Directory
  114800 [     3340] address [size] of Security Directory
  140000 [     46AC] address [size] of Base Relocation Directory
   CF2A4 [       38] address [size] of Debug Directory
       0 [        0] address [size] of Description Directory
       0 [        0] address [size] of Special Directory
       0 [        0] address [size] of Thread Storage Directory
   6CE60 [       40] address [size] of Load Configuration Directory
       0 [        0] address [size] of Bound Import Directory
       0 [        0] address [size] of Import Address Table Directory
       0 [        0] address [size] of Delay Import Directory
       0 [        0] address [size] of COR20 Header Directory
       0 [        0] address [size] of Reserved Directory


SECTION HEADER #1
   .text name
   BF303 virtual size
   10000 virtual address
   BF400 size of raw data
     400 file pointer to raw data
       0 file pointer to relocation table
```

```
            0 file pointer to line numbers
            0 number of relocations
            0 number of line numbers
     60000020 flags
             Code
             (no align specified)
             Execute Read


Debug Directories(2)
          Type      Size      Address   Pointer
Can't read debug dir

SECTION HEADER #2
          RT name
         18C virtual size
       D0000 virtual address
         200 size of raw data
       BF800 file pointer to raw data
            0 file pointer to relocation table
            0 file pointer to line numbers
            0 number of relocations
            0 number of line numbers
     60000020 flags
             Code
             (no align specified)
             Execute Read

SECTION HEADER #3
       .data name
        A6FD virtual size
       E0000 virtual address
        7A00 size of raw data
       BFA00 file pointer to raw data
            0 file pointer to relocation table
            0 file pointer to line numbers
            0 number of relocations
            0 number of line numbers
     C0000040 flags
             Initialized Data
             (no align specified)
             Read Write

SECTION HEADER #4
       .rsrc name
       48BC0 virtual size
       F0000 virtual address
       48C00 size of raw data
       C7400 file pointer to raw data
            0 file pointer to relocation table
            0 file pointer to line numbers
            0 number of relocations
            0 number of line numbers
     40000040 flags
             Initialized Data
             (no align specified)
             Read Only

SECTION HEADER #5
       .reloc name
        46AC virtual size
      140000 virtual address
        4800 size of raw data
      110000 file pointer to raw data
            0 file pointer to relocation table
            0 file pointer to line numbers
            0 number of relocations
```

```
       0 number of line numbers
42000040 flags
         Initialized Data
         Discardable
         (no align specified)
         Read Only
```

Further Reading (Patterns)

- The Timeless Way of Building (by Christopher Alexander)

- A Pattern Language: Towns, Buildings, Construction (by Christopher Alexander, et al.)

© 2014 Software Diagnostics Institute

Here are some links for further reading about the pattern language approach. In these 2 books a pattern language was systematically introduced for architecture and building in the late 70s.

Further Reading (MDA)

- Cloud Memory Dump Analysis

- Fundamentals of Physical Memory Analysis

- Victimware

- Pattern-Oriented Software Forensics

- Debugging TV

© 2014 Software Diagnostics Institute

Here are links to memory dump analysis presentations which are also applicable to memory forensics. Many Debugging TV episodes also cover memory analysis and tools such as WinDbg from Debugging Tools for Windows.

Cloud Memory Dump Analysis:

http://www.patterndiagnostics.com/CMDA-materials

Fundamentals of Physical Memory Analysis:

http://www.patterndiagnostics.com/FPMA-materials

Victimware:

http://www.patterndiagnostics.com/Victimware-materials

Pattern-Oriented Software Forensics:

http://www.patterndiagnostics.com/pattern-oriented-software-forensics-materials

Debugging TV:

http://www.debugging.tv/

Further Reading (SD)

- Software Diagnostics Institute

- Pattern-Driven Software Diagnostics

- Systemic Software Diagnostics

- Pattern-Based Software Diagnostics

- Philosophy of Software Diagnostics

© 2014 Software Diagnostics Institute

Here are some links for further reading about pattern-oriented software diagnostics which can serve as a foundation for pattern-oriented memory forensics. Most of them are presentations with recordings and transcripts published as books.

Software Diagnostics Institute:

http://www.dumpanalysis.org

Pattern-Driven Software Diagnostics:

http://www.patterndiagnostics.com/Introduction-Software-Diagnostics-materials

Systemic Software Diagnostics:

http://www.patterndiagnostics.com/systemic-diagnostics-materials

Pattern-Based Software Diagnostics:

http://www.patterndiagnostics.com/pattern-based-diagnostics-materials

Philosophy of Software Diagnostics:

http://www.patterndiagnostics.com/philosophy-diagnostics-materials

Current Reference

Memory Dump Analysis Anthology: 7 volumes + 3 colour volumes

Volume 8 is planned for 2015/2016

© 2014 Software Diagnostics Institute

This is a current pattern reference. The 7 volumes have more than 3,000 pages and mostly devoted to memory dump analysis and case studies.

Forthcoming Reference

A Pattern Language for Software Diagnostics, Forensics, and Prognostics: Memory, Traces, Deconstruction (10 volumes)

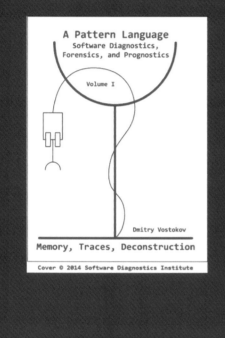

© 2014 Software Diagnostics Institute

Memory Dump Analysis Anthology is now restructured as a pattern language reference with a title **"A Pattern Language for Software Diagnostics, Forensics, and Prognostics: Memory, Traces, Deconstruction"** with projected 10 volumes.